HOW TO LISTEN TO THE UNIVERSE

(Aether downloads)

MARCO J. WILLIAMS

TABLE OF CONTENTS

PREFACE

Welcome to an extraordinary video game experience! In this unique virtual world, your mission as the player is to guide your avatar toward the realization that they are merely characters in a game. This challenge is both intriguing and complex, but fear not, as you possess the power to aid your avatar on this self-discovery journey using special nudges known as synchronicities.

While the avatar embarks on their quest, they must navigate through a world filled with antagonists whose sole purpose is to hinder their path to self-awareness. These powerful distractions manifest in the avatar's everyday life, making the task all the more challenging. Nevertheless, your unwavering persistence ensures that you continuously offer synchronicities, gently pushing the avatar toward enlightenment. As your avatar encounters these synchronicities day after day, their intuition begins to blossom, and they start to notice the recurring patterns. This heightened intuition serves as a key turning point in the game, granting you the ability to communicate directly with the avatar. With this newfound connection, the avatar gains control over the game, allowing them to shape their reality as they desire. However, this revelation is not the end of the game. Instead, a new daunting task awaits your avatar—to help all the other characters within the game come to the same profound realization. As you guide each avatar towards self-awareness, they begin to understand that they are all interconnected with you, the player. The game reaches its ultimate conclusion when every character acknowledges this profound truth and recognizes their connection to you.

This captivating journey reminds us that the game's beauty lies not just in the destination but also in the connections we make along the way. So, immerse yourself in this adventure and let the power of synchronicities guide your avatar and their virtual companions towards self-discovery and unity.

CHAPTER ONE

PAYING ATTENTION TO THE PATTERNS

Greetings, exalted ones. I welcome you to a journey to explore the vast expanse of the universe. When we ponder the universe, what thoughts come to mind? Perhaps stars, planets, and an unending expanse of space? If so, you would indeed be correct. By definition, the universe encompasses all of space and time, including celestial bodies such as planets, stars, galaxies, and the entirety of matter and energy.

However, when I contemplate the Universe, I envision a boundless reservoir of energy that permeates everything. Each day, the Universe presents us with signs, communicating through frequency, vibration, and patterns. These signs manifest as repeating numbers, intuitive thoughts, and premonitions—what I like to call "Downloads." Unfortunately, many people fail to notice these subtle messages due to the incessant distractions of the life we refer to as the matrix.

So, let us venture forth and delve deeper into the enigmatic secrets that the Universe has to offer. By paying heed to these downloads, we may unlock the hidden wisdom and purpose that lies within the fabric of existence.

AETHER DOWNLOADS

In a computer-oriented analogy, a download refers to the act or process of receiving data. From a metaphysical point of view, downloads are the daily information that emanates from the aether, encompassing various aspects of the universe's workings.

Renowned theoretical physicist and University of Maryland Professor, Dr. Jim Gates, devoted his entire career to the pursuit of supersymmetry. During his research, he made a groundbreaking revelation that the entire universe operates based on a specific code known as the Adinkra code. Adinkras serve as visual representations of complex mathematical equations in physics.

What truly astonished Dr. Gates was the omnipresence of certain codes. He used the example of internet browser programs, which contain error-correcting code. Surprisingly, these very same codes underlie the functioning of search engines and web browsers, and similarly, they govern the entire universe. Dr. Gates invites us to consider a fascinating scenario: Imagine being a scientist within an immense virtual computer. The only way to ascertain that your reality is not the ultimate reality is to recognize that your existence is embedded in codes. This understanding prompts you to search for patterns within the fabric of physics.

In essence, our reality can be likened to a computer code, akin to the concept portrayed in the 1999 movie "The Matrix." By recognizing the underlying code, we gain deeper insights into the fundamental nature of the universe and the intricacies that govern its functioning.

Neo's journey represents the universal quest for self-awareness and liberation from the confines of the digital veil. The protagonist, an unwitting player, is drawn to seek the truth behind the veil of illusion that shrouds his consciousness. The downloads he receives are akin to whispers from the architects of this reality, gentle nudges intended to awaken his dormant potential and guide him toward the realization of his true nature. Each download, a burst of celestial light that cascades through Neo's consciousness, bestows him with revelations, skills, and understanding. They represent moments of profound insight when he deciphers the underlying code that governs the illusions of his existence. Just as knowledge shapes and empowers Neo's journey, enlightenment in our own reality stems from the acquisition of wisdom and comprehension of the underlying fabric of existence.

The veil of the matrix serves as a reminder that reality is often not what it seems. Just as the illusion of the digital world initially blinds Neo, so also are we blinded by the veils of perceptions and conditioned beliefs that obscure our understanding of the profound interconnectedness of all things.

As we venture on our own quests for truth and self-discovery, we begin to peel back the layers of deception, ultimately realizing that our reality is an intricate web of codes. The matrix becomes a canvas of possibilities where the understanding of this code grants us the power to shape our own destinies and transcend the limitations that once bound us. The influx of downloads into our lives takes various forms, with thoughts being one of the significant channels.

Sometimes, these thoughts can be weighty, keeping us awake at night as we toss and turn. Embedded within these profound ruminations lies a message that emerges from our subconscious mind. To liberate these messages and gain clarity, one effective approach is to put pen to paper and write them down, gathering and preserving them. Think of your thoughts as scattered Lego pieces on the floor—an initial jumble. Yet, as you calm your mind and take the time to follow the instructions, you begin piecing them together, ultimately creating a masterpiece.

In this context, the masterpiece symbolizes the message hidden within your thoughts, and the instructions represent the guidance that leads you to access the downloads from the aether—the universal wellspring of information and wisdom. Through this process of introspection and reflection, you uncover profound insights and revelations that can illuminate your path and enrich your understanding of existence.

ANGEL NUMBERS

Angel numbers are a concept associated with numerology and spirituality. According to this belief, angels or spiritual beings communicate with humans through repetitive number sequences or patterns known as angel numbers. These numbers are believed to convey specific messages and guidance from the divine realm. The universe loves to communicate through repetition, and what better way to do so than through numbers? After all, math is considered the universal language. During the start of a spiritual journey, many people begin to notice angel numbers, such as 11:11, 2:22, or 4:44, among others. However, angel numbers can have different meanings for different people. If you are seeing these synchronicities, it is because the universe is working with you, trying to guide you through a particular phase of your life.

In 2018, I was invited to participate in a game show called the Misery Index, which was filmed in New York City. While I was at Penn Station, I decided to stop at a store to grab a bite to eat. There, a homeless man approached me and said, "Hey man, I don't want any money. I'm just hungry. Can you help me out with some food?" Of course, I helped him out; I would have wanted someone to do the same for me if I were in his shoes. I told him to order whatever he wanted, and he gratefully asked for a cheese steak and a drink. As he couldn't stop thanking me, I replied, "It's all good; enjoy your meal."

Just before throwing away the receipt for his meal, I happened to glance at the total. It was exactly $8.88. At that moment, I felt that a blessing was on its way. And indeed, within two hours of that interaction, I ended up winning $20,000.

It seemed that by putting out good karma, the universe rewarded me. It was as if the universe had spoken to me, telling me that it would reward me with that receipt. The repeating 8s, which symbolize an abundance of success and prosperity, started to appear more frequently in my life. For instance, in 2020, around the time of the COVID-19 pandemic, I created a second TikTok account, which quickly gained a massive following. Within a few months, I reached half a million followers.Although I had set a goal to reach one million followers by the year's end, TikTok had other plans. My account was deleted when I reached 888,000 followers due to community guideline violations. Initially, I was devastated, feeling like I had lost my voice and my platform was gone, leaving the world unable to hear me anymore. However, little did I know that this was all part of the divine plan. TikTok's action allowed me to refocus and rebrand my content strategy, aligning it with the path the universe intended for me. During this time, I had the opportunity to reflect on the signs and let the thoughts sink in. A voice in my head urged me to "start posting on YouTube and Facebook."

I heeded the guidance and created another TikTok account, this time sharing content that directed people to my YouTube channel. In a matter of months, my YouTube channel gained over twenty thousand followers, while my Facebook page attracted over one hundred thousand followers.

Additionally, my new TikTok account grew to over half a million followers. As my follower count increased, so did my bank account. YouTube and Facebook provided opportunities to monetize my content, and the number '888' continued to bless me.

Now that you've seen what repeating 8s means to me, let's explore the meanings of other angel numbers so you can correlate them with what's happening in your life.

111

Let's start with the number 1. Most people look at a clock when it hits 11:11 and make a wish. But why 11:11? One is a very powerful number; seeing a repeating set of ones represents a divine meaning of awareness.

111 is connected to creativity and individuality; this can be related to the divine masculine and divine feminine balance. Your intentions are manifesting quicker than normal; your thoughts can become your reality, whether those thoughts are good or bad. For example, if someone brake-checks you on the highway, you get angry and want to pull up next to them and curse them out. You look at their license plate, and you see 111. That rage you wanted to let out could be the universe's way of letting you know that you're attracting negative things in your life. The brake check was your guide's way of letting you know that you're vibrating high or low and you need to re-center. Pay attention to whatever you're thinking or feeling whenever you see any angel number.

222

Now, let's get into seeing a repeating set of 2's. Let's say you're sitting outside the office for a job that you really want. You glance over at the clock and see the time is 2:22 pm. This is a good indication that you will more than likely be hired. The number 2 is ruled by the moon and represents harmony and balance. This message is the universe's way of reminding you that you're in the right place at the right time. You should be open to receiving whatever blessing is about to enter your life. It could be a new relationship after a period of loneliness or an amazing opportunity. Take it all in, and remember that everything is going as planned.

333

The number 3 is a powerful number; it represents the divine trinity. Number three, by itself, is associated with creativity, self-expression, and communication. In astrology, the third sign is Gemini, known as the sign of communication.

A person with a life path of 3 is surrounded by creativity, artistry, and the ability to bring things to life. These individuals are often entertainers, artists, and poets. They tend to be the life of the party, viewing life as their stage. Examples of people with a life path of three are Kevin Hart, Snoop Dogg & Katy Perry.

Seeing repeating 3s means you are being supported by beings of an even higher dimension. This usually occurs when you're functioning on a high vibration. You are at a stage in your life where it is very beneficial to create something new and nurture it into completion.

444

There are four seasons, four elements, and four cycles of life. What does the number 4 mean to you? For me, it holds significant meaning as I was born on the 4th of September. When I first joined the fire department, fate led me to Station 4 Catonsville, my very first station.

I cherished my time there—the historic station, the camaraderie on Frederick Road Fridays, and the overall vibe of Catonsville. However, I knew good shifts couldn't last forever due to promotions, but I embraced the moment with my fellow firefighters. We supported each other in pursuing our goals and held each other accountable to our true potential. That's the beauty of the Number 4.

Number 4 signifies grounding and stability, representing traits such as perseverance, patience, hard work, dedication, and honesty. It reminds us to be present and live in the now, focusing on building a strong foundation and maintaining a down-to-earth perspective.

If you constantly encounter the number 4, it might be a sign to examine your foundation. Is it solid, or does it need some work? Remember, angel numbers are unique to each individual and their life circumstances. It's crucial to be aware of how your thoughts and actions influence your spiritual journey.

Angel number 4 encourages you to seize opportunities to fulfill your life's purpose. When you take positive actions aligned with your divine mission, the universe conspires in your favor. The appearance of 444 is a gentle reminder that you have nothing to fear. All is well; let go of your doubts and surrender to the universe.

555

The number 5 is the number of change. There's something mysterious about the number 5, and it seems to have a profound connection to your life. When you notice this synchronicity, it might be a sign that a specific area of your life requires some changes. Change can be either positive or negative, depending on how well we embrace and adapt to it. For those who are open and accustomed to change, it can be a transformative experience akin to evolution itself. The universe seems to use the number 5 to send a message that it's time to switch things up and break away from mundane routines. A personal experience that exemplifies this phenomenon is when I observed my uncle's life. He had fallen into a repetitive cycle: waking up early every morning to go for a run, heading to work via the Long Island Railroad, working long hours, and returning home only to repeat the same routine the next day. Weekends offered little excitement, with Saturdays being uneventful and Sundays dedicated to preparing for the week ahead while watching football.

Amid his monotonous life, he encountered his now-wife, and on the day of their wedding, the clock showed 5:55 pm, as if time itself were hinting at a turning point. Although this change didn't directly impact me, witnessing someone close to me transform their life was remarkable. Eventually, he moved out of his one-bedroom apartment. He found happiness with his wonderful wife, who prepared him home-cooked meals and accompanied him on exciting journeys around the world—his weekends ceased to be uneventful as they now embraced new adventures together.

The number 5 represents change, expansion, and versatility. When angel numbers like this appear in your life, it's essential to reflect on the current state of your life and be open to the idea of change. Embracing change can lead to positive transformations and opportunities for growth.

Remember, the universe might be gently nudging you towards making changes in your life, and it's up to you to recognize these signs and embrace the potential for positive evolution. So, take a step back, analyze your life, and welcome change with open arms, knowing that it can lead to wonderful new experiences and adventures.

666

We have all been indoctrinated to be afraid of the number 666; many believe it is a reference to the mark of the beast. However, if you were to look at the periodic table and take the 6th element, you would notice that Carbon-12 is a specific isotope of carbon, and it is the most abundant and stable form of carbon found in nature. C-12 contains 6 protons, 6 electrons, and 6 neutrons.

Carbon is an essential element found in all living organisms and is a fundamental building block of organic compounds. Its abundance and stability make it a key element for life as we know it. Humans operate in this 3D realm in the flesh; the flesh is our lowest form, hence why it is known as "The mark of the beast." Humans are the beast.

Your root chakra is your lowest form. If you are constantly seeing 666, it could mean you are operating at your lowest form. This could be a reminder to stop acting out of low-vibration emotions, such as fear, hate, greed, and gluttony. It's time for you to step into your higher divine self. Stop being preoccupied by the materialistic things that keep you human. Listen to your intuition and detach from your materialistic world. When you stop worrying about these materialistic things, you will be rewarded abundantly.

The number 6 is associated with the planet Venus; it represents wealth, beauty, art, and creativity. The universe will reward you when you shift your focus; you must elevate into your higher chakras, such as your heart, and have a service to others.

777

The number 7 holds significant spiritual importance among the numbers from 1 to 9. In numerology, the number 7 is ruled by Neptune and symbolizes deep spiritual wisdom. It carries an internal essence that resonates with profound spiritual insights.

In the United States, many gamblers believe 777 to be a lucky number, often associating it with jackpot wins on slot machines. If you repeatedly encounter the number 7, it might serve as a prompt to take a risk, especially if an opportunity presents itself that seems a little daring.

The universe is sending a message that luck and abundance are on your side. However, on the flip side, it could also be a reminder that amassing material wealth should not be your sole focus. It may be time to let go of addictions and bad habits, directing your attention towards more meaningful and spiritually fulfilling endeavors.

888

The 2008 Olympic Games held in Beijing, China, started in the 8th month of the year at 8:08 pm. Within two years, China became the world's second-largest economy. On April 25th, 2022, Twitter's board accepted Elon Musk's $44 Billion takeover bid. In numerology, 04/25/2022 is an 8-day period. You might be thinking that the math isn't adding up until you break it down like this: $4 + 2 + 5 + 2 + 2 + 2 = 17$, and then $1 + 7 = 8$.

As part of Elon Musk's takeover, he stated that he would charge Twitter users $8 per month for a blue tick indicating a verified account. The number 8 is associated with money, power, planning, karma, and abundance, encompassing a wide range of blessings, from financial wealth to family and influence.

Interestingly, the number 8 is shaped like the infinity symbol, symbolizing the concept of what goes around, comes around. Earlier in this angel number series, I mentioned how I gave food to a homeless man, and the receipt for his meal came to $8.88. This act of good karma was rewarded with an abundance of financial blessings because that's the power of the energy associated with the number 8.

999

The number 9 holds a unique significance as it is the last of the single-digit numbers and encompasses the energies of all the previous numbers. Symbolically, 9 represents completion, indicating that a certain chapter of your life is reaching its conclusion, and you are evolving from it.

I have a personal connection with the number 9, as I was assigned to Station 9 during the end of my one-and-a-half-year relationship with my kid's mother. When that chapter of my life came to completion, I went through a transformative process. In the following year 2020, I was promoted, and I embarked on a soul-searching journey. And a year later, while going through this transition, it eventually led me to my current partner. She has been instrumental in guiding me on my path of growth and evolution.

When you repeatedly encounter the number 9, it serves as a reminder to move forward. Whatever has come to an end was meant to end, making way for a new chapter in your life. The number 9 encourages you not to remain stagnant but to ascend to your highest self. Unlike the number 6, which tends to spiral down to your lower chakras, the energy of 9 spirals upward, elevating your consciousness. What's fascinating about the number 9 is that it remains undiminished in power when multiplied by other numbers.

Table	Sum of the digits of each product
1 x 9 = 9	0 + 9 = 9
2 x 9 = 18	1 + 8 = 9
3 x 9 = 27	2 + 7 = 9
4 x 9 = 36	3 + 6 = 9
5 x 9 = 45	4 + 5 = 9
6 x 9 = 54	5 + 4 = 9
7 x 9 = 63	6 + 3 = 9
8 x 9 = 72	7 + 2 = 9
9 x 9 = 81	8 + 1 = 9
10 x 9 = 90	9 + 0 = 9

9 retains its unique essence and represents an unyielding force of completion and transformation. In the numerical realm, there is no number higher than 9; all other numbers like 10, 11, 12, and so on are compound numbers derived from the digits 0-9.

The universe is said to vibrate at a frequency of 432 Hz, which interestingly equals 9 on addition: $4 + 3 + 2 = 9$. Numbers hold intrinsic value and carry unique vibrations. Our entire universe is built upon the foundation of numbers, and 9 stands as the highest vibrational single-digit number (excluding double master numbers). It signifies fulfillment and embodies divine wisdom within this 3D realm over which it governs.

CHAPTER TWO

MANIFESTATION

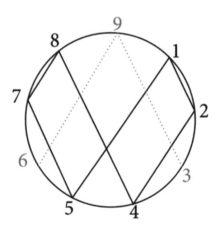

The power of 3, 6, 9 *"If you only knew the magnificence of the 3, 6, and 9, then you would have the key to the universe."*
Nikola Tesla

Nikola Tesla was obsessed with the numbers 3, 6, and 9. He would make calculations about things in his immediate surroundings to ensure that the results were divisible by 3, and he would then base his choices based on those results. He would do everything in sets of three. From living in hotel rooms, divisible by three, or walking around the block three times before entering his apartment. He would even clean his plate six times. But why these numbers? What was Tesla trying to make the world understand?

After learning about Tesla's quirky fascination with the numbers 3, 6, and 9, I decided to incorporate this concept into my life. This realization coincided with the beginning of my fitness journey, during which I set a goal to gain 20 lbs. In my workout routine, I integrated drop sets of 3, 6, and 9 repetitions. The first set involved 9 reps. With a lighter weight, followed by a set of 6 reps with increased weight, and finally, the third set of 3 reps with the heaviest weight. To support my workout efforts, I aimed to exercise at least six times a week while consuming over six thousand calories daily. Most of my calorie intake came from serious mass protein shakes, with each shake consisting of three servings totaling 1000 calories throughout the day. Within just three months of adopting this approach, I noticed significant improvements in both my strength and size. As I admired my progress in the mirror, I began to develop a genuine affection for this journey. The gym became a sanctuary for me, a place where I cherished every moment and shaped myself mentally, physically and spiritually.

I learned that true manifestation and creation stem from being in the present moment, embracing the journey, and cultivating gratitude. This realization was merely the beginning of my manifestation journey. I delved deeper into understanding how the universe communicates through energy and vibration, where everything, from plants to crystals to humans, vibrates at its unique frequency. In order to attract something, one must resonate with its frequency. Have you ever noticed how certain individuals effortlessly attract animals? It's because they know how to connect with their frequency. This principle applies to everything in life. Our thoughts and emotions generate energy, which exists in a state of vibration. For effective manifestation, it's essential to document your desires. I recommend obtaining a manifestation journal dedicated to capturing your aspirations. Write them down three times in the morning, six times in the evening, and nine times at night. This practice is the power behind the 369 method.

ALIGNING WITH YOUR AFFIRMATIONS

There are several manifestation methods available, such as the scripting method, the whisper method, and the 1 2 3 method. While we won't delve into each method here, the fundamental principles remain the same.

When writing your manifestations, it's crucial to express them in the present tense because the future does not yet exist. Avoid framing your manifestations as mere desires, as the universe doesn't reward desires. For instance, phrases like "I want," "I hope," or "I wish" fall into the category of desires. For example, wishing at 11:11 may yield no results because it is merely a desire. Instead, structure your affirmations like this:

- "I have the best position in the company."
- "I possess my dream home in the perfect neighborhood."
- "I am grateful for my growth in life."

Once you declare these affirmations, release them to the universe because you already possess what you desire. In my personal experience, the last time I manifested money was in 2018. During this time, I found myself being irresponsible with my finances and accumulating debt with no clear plan to pay it off. However, I had a realization that compelled me to take action: "I need to pay this off."

I decided to write a note to myself, stating my intention to pay off the debt within six years. At that moment, I had no idea where the money would come from, but I held unwavering faith that it would come.

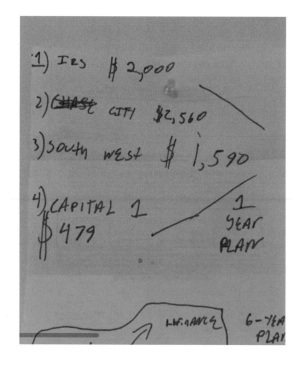

In August 2018, I took a picture of all my debt and hung it up in my closet, affirming that I would pay it off. Writing down my happiness for being able to provide for my family without being enslaved by debt, I visualized a debt-free life in my mind's eye and began to truly believe it.

Two months later, I received a direct message on Instagram from a producer of a show called The Misery Index. The producer offered me the opportunity to participate in a game show and meet the Impractical Jokers, whom I loved watching. While meeting them was never something I imagined, I did envision an abundance of money coming into my life. Out of nowhere, this opportunity came to me.

During the first interview, the producer asked me to share an embarrassing story to see if I could relate to the Impractical Jokers' style. Though I had no idea what I was getting into, I recounted the time in middle school when I had an unfortunate episode of diarrhea. I shared how it happened at school, and I had to ride home on the bus with it on my shirt, making for an incredibly awkward experience. This story was good enough to proceed to a secondary Facetime interview with other producers who loved my personality and eventually invited me onto the show. After months of paperwork and preparation, I finally arrived in New York. On the way, I encountered the homeless man mentioned earlier in chapter one. Once on the set, they were filming a segment of men versus women. As one of only two guys among four women, I felt confident that I had a good chance of being selected since they were only filming two shows that day.

During the first half of the show, I was losing badly, but deep down, I knew it wasn't my destiny to lose.

After everything was said and done, I ended up winning $20,000. However, this was not the end of my manifestation journey. The universe blessed me in a unique way through a series of unfortunate events. In August 2022, I experienced a car accident that led to the complete destruction of my Jeep. Regrettably, the decision to buy the jeep was driven by a desire for showiness, opting for a striking purple color. In hindsight, this choice became a significant financial burden rather than a source of satisfaction. Despite the devastation I felt due to its sentimental value, I received a payout of over $24,000 from the insurance company. Taking a step back and looking at the bigger picture, I realized that the car had served its purpose in my life, and this was all part of my manifestation. It was remarkable to see that even though I had made this manifestation years ago, it had still come to fruition. I had been stressing out about the situation without realizing that it was all part of the journey and a blessing. I had manifested a life free of debt, and that's exactly what I received. All it took was an aligned thought, gratitude, and surrendering to the universe.

Now, let's discuss the issue of manifesting materialistic things like money. Money is considered fake in the sense that it is a man-made construct, and focusing solely on manifesting money can lead to a continuous cycle of manifestation. Manifesting money can distract from the true essence of manifestation, which is about manifesting an outcome and embracing the process, not just manifesting the process itself and accepting the outcome.

The most crucial aspect of manifestation is the process. Being present and embracing the journey is where the lessons are learned. Remember that the purpose of manifestation is to manifest your highest self, not merely tangible things that serve your physical existence. Always prioritize serving the soul rather than the desires of the flesh. You are not just a body; you are a soul with a conscience. Your consciousness serves as the context for the content of the reality you create.

Your thoughts are powerful! Your thoughts equal the energy that is projected into the aether. You are the power behind the thought that decides whether or not the thought is true for you. Any thoughts that you don't want to be true should be immediately canceled out when they cross your mind. Reject them promptly because they do not serve your highest self. Likewise, embrace the thoughts that serve you. We perceive reality based on our past programming. What you imprint on your subconscious plays out in your daily life. If you consciously decide to imprint what you want to see happening in your life, whatever you're chasing should also chase you. That's how alignment works—the principle of mentalism.

"The All is Mind; the Universe is Mental." **The Kybalion**

Through this principle, it is believed that God is consciousness or thought, and the universe is a manifestation of the mind of God. Using this law, we can harness the power of our minds to create the life we desire. We are the universe experiencing itself in human form. Each person will have their own perceptions and beliefs that can distort the truth. To get back to the truth, we have to reset to a state of emptiness. We can achieve this by meditating, similar to resetting a computer back to its factory settings. The mind is empty; there is no "my mind" or "your mind"; there is only one mind: the all or nothing in it. When you combine this law with the principle of correspondence: "As above, so below; as below, so above." **The Kybalion,** then you understand that if God is the creator and we were created in the image of God, our mind is similar to the divine mind, and thus we can create a reflection. The knowledge of these two principles forms the foundation of manifestation

The best way to empty our minds is through meditation. Though we won't delve too deeply into meditation in this chapter, we will address how it's a critical step when it comes to manifestation. One should practice meditation before practicing manifestation. Manifestation requires you to paint the picture first, and you can achieve that through receptive meditation. Receptive meditation quiets the mind and allows you to connect to the intelligence of the universe, bringing it into this reality. When the universe, God, or your higher self reveals information to you, it's up to you to bring it into reality through active meditation.

Active meditation has the power to open the heart and emit a higher frequency that removes all limiting beliefs and blocks that might be hindering your manifestation from coming to fruition. As you begin to incorporate both active and passive meditation, everything will naturally fall into place because you are no longer blocking the higher frequencies that come through from your higher self.

CHAPTER THREE

MEDITATION

TAPPING INTO THE FREQUENCY LINE

Meditation is a state of being that enables individuals to connect with the frequency line of the universe. The universe is composed of energy, vibrations, and interconnectedness. Through meditation, one may attune one's consciousness to these cosmic frequencies. At its core, meditation is a practice that involves turning one's attention inward, quieting the mind, and being fully present in the moment. By doing so, meditators seek to transcend the limitations of the physical body and ego. This allows them to access deeper realms of consciousness. In this state, they may perceive themselves as a part of the vast cosmic web connected to everything that exists. To understand meditation as tapping into the frequency line of the universe, one can use the analogy of a radio receiver .Just as a radio receiver tunes into specific frequencies to pick up different radio stations, meditation enables individuals to attune their minds to higher or subtler frequencies. These frequencies may represent the underlying fabric of the universe, carrying information and knowledge beyond what is accessible through ordinary sensory perceptions.

Through consistent and disciplined meditation, practitioners may experience a shift in their awareness, feeling a sense of unity with all that is tangible and intangible. This heightened state of consciousness allows them to tap into the universal flow of energy and information, helping them to gain insights and wisdom that extend beyond the boundaries of their individual selves. In essence, they realize that they are not separate entities but rather interconnected with all living beings and the entire cosmos. This awareness promotes a sense of unity, compassion, and empathy for others and the world around them.

As individuals align with the frequencies of the universe, they may access profound insights and intuitive understandings that go beyond the limitations of rational thinking. This wisdom may guide them in making choices that align with their true purpose and contribute to the greater good. The universe is considered to be an infinite reservoir of energy. Meditation can be seen as a means of channeling and harmonizing with this energy, fostering a sense of vitality and well-being.

Through meditation, practitioners may experience an expansion of their consciousness, transcending the limitations of the individual ego and gaining access to a broader, more profound aspect of themselves and the universe. Just like tuning a musical instrument to vibrate in harmony with a specific pitch, meditation may help individuals attune their consciousness to resonate with the fundamental frequencies of existence.

> "Every genius thinks INWARDLY toward his Mind instead of outwardly toward his senses. The genius can hear sounds coming out of the silence with his inner ears. He can vision non-existent forms with his inner eyes and he can feel the rhythms of God's thinking and His knowing—which are a blank slate to the man who believes that HE is his body. When a human rises to the exalted state of genius, he becomes a co-Creator with God." —**Walter Russell**

MEDITATION IS A DIET; FIND WHAT WORKS FOR YOU

Many people might find it surprising, but a crucial step in meditation is to listen to everything that's going on inside and outside. The experience can be overwhelming because our minds are bombarded with numerous thoughts from everyday life, including thoughts about past and future events that have not yet happened.

However, meditation is a powerful tool that can help us learn to sort through all the mental noise and avoid becoming prisoners to our own thoughts. Interestingly, some individuals might claim they don't know how to sit down and meditate, but in reality, most people meditate every day without even realizing it. Meditation can manifest in various forms, such as putting oneself in a state of flow or being "in the zone." The flow state involves being fully absorbed in an activity, where complete focus is on the task at hand, and nothing else matters at that moment. During this state, people often experience a sense of euphoria, and time may seem to either speed up or slow down, occasionally causing one to lose track of it. Writers, artists, musicians, and athletes are among those who tap into this space, allowing them to block out their current reality and access their inner genius.

Your space of creation can become your meditation. Meditation has the potential to unlock joy and creativity from within. By practicing meditation, you can train your mind to be less receptive to distractions, thereby allowing it to reveal more of its conscious self. Now, take a moment to ask yourself, "What is it that allows me to tap into myself?" Comparatively, meditation can be likened to a diet; just as we all have different body types, what helps one person maintain their weight may not work for another. Thus, you need to find what works best for you. There are numerous meditation techniques, which we will address later in this chapter. For some, meditation may occur in the shower, while others might find it through listening to music or going on a long drive and completely zoning out. The key is to explore and discover the meditation practices that resonate with you and enable you to reach a state of inner peace and clarity.

Starting meditation can be challenging, especially when learning to quiet your thoughts. However, like anything in life, it takes practice. Imagine your mind as a bustling train station, with thoughts being the trains arriving and departing. The goal is not to hop on every train that pulls into the station; instead, you're aiming to board a specific train that will take you to a certain destination. To avoid getting lost in every thought and maintain focus, find an object of meditation. This could be the sound of birds chirping, sensations in the body, or even your own breathing. Utilizing the calming sound of your breath, a natural gift from mother nature, can be particularly effective.

Whenever your mind starts to wander, gently redirect it back to the chosen object of meditation. When I began my meditation journey, I started with guided meditations on YouTube. I recommend beginners to use guides as they offer a better understanding of how to quiet the mind effectively.

An app called "Headspace" also worked wonders for me. Developed by Andy Puddicombe, a former Buddhist Monk, the app serves as a daily reminder to dedicate time to meditation, a crucial escape from the chaos of life. For me, the most powerful meditation sessions occur whenever I immerse myself in nature. During the pandemic of 2020, I took up hiking and discovered that long walks surrounded by trees and the sound of birds helped relax my mind and clear my thoughts. In the past, my attempts to meditate often failed because I struggled to silence my mind. I allowed my thoughts to overrun every session. However, I eventually realized that the process of meditation involves acknowledging and releasing these thoughts, allowing suppressed subconscious thoughts to surface.

There are various types of meditation, each serving different purposes and benefiting different aspects of life. My personal favorite is mindful meditation, which proved to be therapeutic in dealing with everyday stress and anxiety. Through this practice, I found myself reacting less negatively to external circumstances, even when faced with frustrating situations like road rage or being stuck in traffic while running late. I cultivated a natural state of acceptance and understanding that everything unfolds as it's meant to, and eventually, things will resolve themselves.

Meditation is a powerful tool that can be tailored to suit individual preferences and needs. With regular practice and patience, it can transform the way we experience and navigate life, bringing inner peace and clarity. Mindful meditation enabled me to embrace life as it unfolds, fostering gratitude for the present moment and the simple joys it brings.

Mindful meditation is a mental practice that involves focusing one's attention on the present moment without judgment. It's about being fully aware of your thoughts, feelings, bodily sensations, and the surrounding environment. The practice is rooted in ancient Buddhist traditions but has gained popularity in modern times as a secular form of meditation with numerous physical and psychological benefits.

Give it a try right now. Choose a peaceful environment where you won't be disturbed during your meditation session. Sit or lie down in a comfortable position, keeping your back straight. Take a few deep breaths to relax your body and settle your mind. Then, allow your breath to flow naturally and observe the sensations of each inhalation and exhalation. Pay attention to the rise and fall of your abdomen or the feeling of air passing through your nostrils. As you continue to breathe, thoughts will naturally arise. Instead of getting caught up in these thoughts, gently redirect your focus back to your breath. Acknowledge the thoughts without judgment, and then let them pass by, returning your attention to the present moment.

If you find yourself getting distracted or if your mind starts to wander, don't be hard on yourself. It's normal for the mind to wander during meditation. Simply notice that your mind has wandered, and kindly bring your attention back to the breath. After you've spent some time focusing on your breath, you can expand your awareness to other sensations in your body, such as the feeling of the ground beneath you, any tension or relaxation in your muscles, or the sounds around you. Start with short sessions, perhaps minutes, and gradually increase the duration as you become more comfortable with the practice.

Meditation doesn't always require you to be sitting in the lotus position. For those of you who can't sit still, you can try **movement meditation.** Movement meditation is a form of meditation exercise that allows you to shift your mood, process emotions and ease the nervous system. Yoga is the first thing that usually comes to mind when it comes to movement meditation, but movement meditation can include walking/hiking, gardening, Tai chi, qi gong, or other intuitive forms of movement, such as dancing to rhythmic music. If you're someone who doesn't like silence, then **mantra meditation** could be something you should look into. Some people might find it more soothing to repeat a saying like "Om" due to the vibration your body naturally makes while humming it. With mantra meditation, the repetition of the sound specific to you helps the mind and body settle into deeper states of consciousness or a state of rest.

Start by finding a comfortable position, gently close your eyes and take a few deep breaths to relax your body and mind. Start repeating your chosen mantra silently or aloud. Focus your attention on the sound and rhythm of the mantra. If you get lost in thought or distractions, gently bring your awareness back to the mantra. As you continue repeating the mantra, try to let go of any thoughts, worries, or anxieties that arise. Just allow the mantra to be the center of your attention.

You can practice mantra meditation for a specific duration, such as ten, fifteen, or twenty minutes, or for as long as you feel comfortable. Regularity is more important than duration, so try to make it a daily practice. When you're ready to end the meditation, gradually allow the repetition of the mantra to fade away. Take a few deep breaths and sit quietly for a moment before opening your eyes.

The benefits of mantra meditation can include reduced stress, improved focus, increased self-awareness, and a sense of inner peace. Additionally, it can serve as an excellent anchor for your mind when other thoughts try to intrude during your meditation practice.

Another strategy is **body scanning**. It's my go-to meditation whenever I'm sick. Body scanning meditation is a mindfulness technique that involves bringing focused attention to different parts of the body, usually starting from the feet and gradually moving up through the rest of the body. The purpose of this practice is to cultivate awareness of bodily sensations, promote relaxation, and develop a deeper connection with oneself. Body scanning meditation is commonly used to reduce stress, relieve physical tension, and improve overall well-being. This meditation can eliminate tension in the body, improve sleeping habits and help ease addictive habits like smoking and drinking. All that's required is a comfortable space. Start by closing your eyes and focusing on your breath. Next, bring awareness to a specific part of your body. Personally, I like to start from the toes of my feet. Then I focus on the feet as a whole, working up from the bottom of the legs through the knees to the top of the legs, then the legs as a whole. Then move on to the hands, relaxing the arms and shoulders, slowly working my way to the crown of the head. This is a great way to quickly remove the everyday stress and tension pressures of life from the body. In my role as a firefighter, I've observed an increasing prevalence of stress, burnout, and mental health issues. It's evident that these concerns are not unique to firefighting; government workers and individuals in corporate jobs can undoubtedly relate to these challenges as well. To help address these challenges, I believe we all should adopt the practices of meditation in workplace settings.

The work environment often exposes employees to high levels of stress and pressure, leading to decreased productivity and job satisfaction. Meditation techniques, such as mindfulness and deep breathing, have been scientifically proven to reduce stress and anxiety, allowing employees to remain focused, resilient, and emotionally stable in the face of challenges.

Western culture has historically placed a strong emphasis on physical health, with ample resources and attention devoted to medical advancements and physical fitness. However, the significance of mental and spiritual well-being has often been overlooked, leading to a gap in addressing the complexities of human emotions and inner struggles. This oversight is particularly evident in the rising suicide rates. During my career, I experienced the loss of two co-workers through suicide, one of them being from my academy class. Experiencing the loss of two co-workers to suicide, especially one from your own academy class, can be an incredibly challenging and emotional ordeal. Coping with such tragedies requires a strong support system and effective strategies for managing the complex emotions that arise. Meditation has helped me navigate grief, loss, and emotional turmoil.

Implementing meditation into your coping strategy can be a meaningful way to honor the memory of your co-workers while nurturing your own mental and emotional well-being. We have a pressing need to shift our focus towards our inner well-being. If you suffer from PTSD, anxiety, or depression, transcendental meditation could help you see life in a different light.

Transcendental Meditation (TM) is a specific form of meditation that gained popularity in the West during the 1960s and 1970s. It is a technique that involves sitting with one's eyes closed and silently repeating a specific mantra, a word or sound repeated to aid concentration in meditation. TM was introduced to the world by Maharishi Mahesh Yogi, an Indian guru and spiritual leader. He first taught TM publicly in 1955 and gained significant attention when The Beatles, along with other celebrities, began practicing TM and spoke positively about its effects. This led to widespread interest in the technique, and TM became a global phenomenon. The impact of TM on popular culture was profound, particularly during the counterculture movement of the 1960s. Many people were drawn to the idea of seeking spiritual enlightenment and inner peace through a simple meditation practice. The celebrity endorsements and media coverage helped make TM mainstream, attracting people from different walks of life, including artists, musicians, actors, and intellectuals.

TM also played a significant role in bringing Eastern spiritual practices to the Western world, paving the way for the widespread acceptance and popularity of meditation and yoga. Its influence on Western spirituality and the New Age movement is notable. However, it's essential to note that TM has also faced criticism and controversies over the years, mainly related to the commercialization of the practice, the high cost of learning the technique, and the organization's claims and scientific research.

The goal of TM is to achieve a state of deep relaxation and inner peace. This leads practitioners to what is described as a state of "Transcendence" or "Pure consciousness", thinking towards silence, taking the mind to a place where it naturally wants to go. Transcend means to go beyond the range or limits. You're transcending into a deeper level of mind, intellect and ideally greater happiness. Going beyond the field of reality and duality to experience oneness with the creator.

This is how you tap into that inner genius and unlock creativity: Love, pure bliss & tranquility entering the kingdom of heaven that lies within you. Vedas call this "Atman," the innermost self or soul of an individual. The concept of Atman is fundamental to understanding the nature of existence, consciousness, and the self. This involves introspection and contemplation to inquire into the nature of the self. The seeker asks questions like "Who am I?" or "What is the true nature of my existence?" This process aims to go beyond the identification with the temporary physical body and the ever-changing mind. Through meditation, one may experience glimpses of the true nature of the self, leading to the realization of Atman. Getting there by knowing oneself and being it is enlightenment. The mind is always moving in the direction of greater happiness. The nature of inner being is bliss and TM is a tool to get you there.

TM allows practitioners to turn their attention inward, exploring the depths of their own minds. With each meditation session, they may dive deeper, gradually peeling away layers of thoughts, emotions, and distractions to access more profound levels of consciousness.

Think of it as you taking an elevator down into your own mind. The elevator's descent can be likened to the different levels of consciousness. As the elevator moves down, you encounter various floors, each representing a different state of mind or layer of awareness. Individuals may progress through various levels of consciousness, ranging from ordinary waking consciousness to deeper, more profound states of inner silence and self-awareness. Reaching the ground floor or the lowest level of the building represents the pinnacle of the journey to attaining Atman.

Just as an elevator can take you back to the surface after exploring the lower floors, meditation allows practitioners to re-emerge from the depths of their consciousness to the external world. However, unlike a physical elevator, the return journey from meditation often leaves individuals with a greater sense of peace, clarity, and self-awareness, which can positively influence their daily lives and interactions.

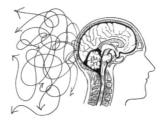

Everyday thoughts good/bad

↓↓
Subtle thoughts
↓↓
Transcendental consciousness
↓↓
Intelligence •Creativity •love • bliss
Atman

Transcendent experiences are events that bring us out of our ordinary minds, making us feel connected to the world around us. Once you experience this state, you've experienced the sweetest nectar of life, pure bliss consciousness. In this state of being, the mind flows with energy, intelligence and happiness. Once you leave this state, you see the beauty this world has to offer.

MEDITATION IS MEDICATION

In a world where pills and prescriptions often dictate our pursuit of well-being, there lies a profound yet often overlooked truth: the mind possesses its own extraordinary capacity for healing. Venturing past the limits of traditional pharmaceuticals, we delve deep into the potential of meditation as an influential remedy for the prevalent afflictions of our modern age. Within the realm of healthcare, meditation is finding an increasingly integral role in treatment regimens. Patients are now receiving meditation practices as part of their "Prescriptions." Similar to a physician determining the appropriate dosage of a drug, meditation instructors prescribe personalized techniques and durations that cater to the unique requirements of each individual.

Meditation offers a different approach, one that aligns mind, body, and spirit. Unlike medications that address symptoms, meditation targets the root causes of distress. It encourages a holistic view of health, emphasizing the interconnectedness of our mental, emotional, and physical well-being. As individuals embark on their meditation journey, they embark on a path toward self-discovery, personal growth, and a deeper understanding of the intricate interplay between their inner and outer worlds.

The potential of meditation to rewire the brain and enhance cognitive and emotional well-being has garnered considerable attention. Multiple research studies have pointed towards the capacity of regular meditation practice to induce both structural and functional changes within the brain. This transformative process ultimately fosters heightened resilience against stress, improved attention spans, and an enhanced ability to regulate emotions. Integral to this phenomenon is the concept of neuroplasticity, the brain's remarkable ability to adapt and reorganize itself. A notable study led by Sarah Lazar and her team at Harvard University stands as a testament to this, revealing that dedicated long-term meditation practitioners displayed an augmentation in gray matter density within brain regions associated with attention, sensory perception, and emotional regulation. These findings illuminate how meditation can potentially exert a positive influence on brain structure, particularly strengthening areas that play a pivotal role in cognitive processes essential for attaining emotional equilibrium and self-awareness.

Furthermore, the research spearheaded by Richard Davidson at the University of Wisconsin-Madison offers deeper insights into meditation's impact on emotional well-being. This study revealed that participants who engaged in an eight-week mindfulness-based meditation program exhibited elevated activity levels in the prefrontal cortex, a brain region intricately tied to positive emotions and comprehensive emotional regulation. This heightened activation coincided with diminished activity within the amygdala, a neural component intricately linked to the processing of adverse emotions like fear and anxiety. These significant findings illuminate the potential of meditation to remodel brain circuitry, steering emotional responses toward a more constructive and balanced state. In summation, these collective research endeavors highlight the remarkable potential of meditation to rewire the brain, presenting an avenue for fortified cognitive functioning, heightened emotional resilience, and holistic well-being.

The practice of regular meditation has been shown to emerge as a potential shield against physical ailments, with studies highlighting a strong connection between meditation and the cultivation of a healthier body. One notable study that demonstrated the profound impact of meditation on cardiovascular health is the "Effects of the Transcendental Meditation Program on Cardiovascular Risk Factors," published in the American Heart Association journal Circulation: Cardiovascular Quality and Outcomes in 2012.

The research was a randomized controlled trial that included 201 African American men and women with coronary heart disease or at high risk for heart disease. The participants were randomly assigned to either a transcendental meditation (TM) group or a health education (HE) group.

The TM group underwent an intensive program to learn the TM technique, while the HE group attended a health education class focused on heart-healthy lifestyle modifications. After one year of intervention, the researchers found significant improvements in several cardiovascular risk factors in the TM group compared to the HE group.

The TM group showed a significant reduction in both systolic and diastolic blood pressure compared to the HE group. Lowering blood pressure is essential for reducing the risk of hypertension and cardiovascular events. The TM group demonstrated a substantial improvement in insulin resistance compared to the HE group.

Reducing insulin resistance is beneficial for managing diabetes and reducing the risk of heart disease. Participants in the TM group reported significant reductions in perceived stress, anxiety, and depression compared to the HE group. The TM group showed a decrease in left ventricular mass compared to the HE group. High left ventricular mass is a risk factor for heart disease.

Emerging research suggests that meditation might also have a profound impact on aging on a cellular level. One of the primary contributors to aging is the shortening of telomeres. The protective caps at the end of chromosomes naturally shrink as cells divide over time. Telomere shortening is associated with cellular aging and increased susceptibility to age-related diseases. Recent studies indicate that regular meditation practices, such as mindfulness and loving-kindness meditation, could potentially slow down this process. The reduction of stress through meditation might play a pivotal role in preserving telomere length and promoting overall cellular health. Moreover, meditation's impact on aging could be attributed to its ability to counteract chronic inflammation, which is closely linked to the aging process. Chronic inflammation is implicated in various age-related diseases, including cardiovascular issues, diabetes, and neurodegenerative disorders. Through relaxation and stress reduction, meditation appears to modulate the body's inflammatory responses, thereby potentially slowing down the detrimental effects of inflammation on tissues and organs. By creating a more balanced immune response, meditation might contribute to healthier aging and an increased lifespan. The extensive advantages of meditation could be discussed endlessly. Clearly, it stands as a form of remedy that holds great potential for enhancing well-being in today's rapid and competitive professional landscape.

Meditation has been practiced for centuries in Eastern cultures as a means to cultivate mental clarity, emotional balance, and spiritual growth. By incorporating meditation practices into our daily lives, individuals can develop a deeper understanding of their thoughts and emotions, learn coping mechanisms for stress, and find a sense of inner peace.

CHAPTER FOUR

CHEAT CODES TO THE UNIVERSE

"Psychedelics are illegal not because a loving government is concerned that you may jump out of a third-story window. Psychedelics are illegal because they dissolve opinion structure and culturally laid down models of behavior and information processing. They open you up to the possibility that everything you know is wrong"
—Terence Mckenna

THE WAR ON DRUGS

In a world of hidden agendas, it should come as no surprise that the ban on psychedelics is not what it seems. Governments around the world have waged a relentless "war on drugs," targeting substances like psychedelics and justifying their prohibition with claims of public health and safety.

The war on drugs has been a powerful tool for governments to exert control over marginalized communities and dissenting voices. By criminalizing drug use, particularly psychedelics, authorities can selectively target individuals and groups they perceive as threats to the existing power structures. This enforcement disproportionately affects minority populations and stifles social movements that challenge the status quo. The prohibition of psychedelics serves the interests of various industries that profit from the criminalization and monopolization of drug-related activities. Law enforcement agencies, private prisons, pharmaceutical companies, and even criminal organizations benefit from the lucrative nature of the black market created by drug prohibition.

The ruling elite thrives on a population that remains docile, ignorant, and easily manipulated. Psychedelics, however, have the power to expand consciousness, leading to critical thinking and increased awareness. This poses a significant threat to those who benefit from a passive and complacent populace, as awakened individuals are more likely to question authority and demand accountability.

Throughout history, many great thinkers, artists, and visionaries have attributed their breakthrough ideas to psychedelic experiences. The ban on psychedelics serves as a means to suppress innovative and revolutionary thinking, preventing the emergence of societal paradigms that challenge the existing power structures. The ruling elite fears the transformative potential of psychedelic-inspired reactivity and its ability to reshape the world. The war on drugs has placed significant legal and financial barriers against scientific and medical research into psychedelics. As a result, the potential benefits of these substances in treating mental health disorders, addiction, and existential distress remain largely untapped. The controlled substances classification hampers scientific progress and prevents the public from accessing alternative, potentially transformative treatments.

By stigmatizing and criminalizing psychedelics, governments miss out on opportunities for harm reduction and education. Prohibition prevents the implementation of quality control measures, proper dosage guidelines, and safe environments for psychedelic experiences. Instead, individuals are left to navigate the underground market, increasing the risk of adulterated substances and unsafe settings. I would like to address that I am not condoning the use of any illicit content. My goal for this chapter is to break the stigmatism associated with cheat codes and give the world a better understanding of the natural gifts the universe provides to access it.

The same information and knowledge that some receive through meditation can also be revealed through certain substances that can show the answers, hence the reason I like to call them "cheat codes." If our reality is a simulation, these cheat codes make us aware that we are the ones in control of our avatar. These cheat codes are naturally produced within us. Some are found all over the world in the form of herbs, mushrooms, cacti, and animals.

HISTORY OF PSYCHEDELICS

Psychedelics, or mind-altering substances, have been used by many ancient cultures throughout history for various purposes, such as religious ceremonies, healing practices, and spiritual exploration. The use of psychedelics dates back thousands of years and is deeply rooted in the history and culture of many societies. However, it is difficult to pinpoint the exact time and place where these substances were first used due to the lack of written records from that time.

One of the earliest known users of psychedelics is believed to be by indigenous cultures in the Americas. The use of Ayahuasca, a powerful psychedelic brew made from plants found in the Amazon rainforest, has been traced back to the ancient Inca civilization in Peru, which flourished between the 13th and 16th centuries. Ayahuasca was used in shamanic rituals as a tool for spiritual insight and healing. In addition to Ayahuasca, other psychedelics, such as peyote and psilocybin mushrooms, were used by indigenous cultures in North and Central America for similar purposes. The use of peyote by Native American tribes such as the Huichol, Navajo, and Apache can be traced back hundreds of years, while the use of psilocybin mushrooms by the Aztecs is documented in their art and literature. Psychedelics were also used in ancient India, where the Hindu God Shiva was said to have consumed a powerful psychoactive substance known as soma to achieve spiritual enlightenment. However, the exact identity of soma is unclear, and it may have been a combination of different plants or substances. There's evidence that suggests that the ancient Egyptians used psychedelics. One of the most famous examples of psychedelic use in ancient Egypt is the blue lotus flower (Nymphaea Caerulea). This plant was known to the ancient Egyptians as "Sacred Lotus" and was used for its psychoactive properties. This plant was often depicted in Egyptian art. It was believed to have healing properties as well as being a potent aphrodisiac.

The blue lotus flower was also used to create tea and wine that the ancient Egyptians consumed. The effects of the plant are said to be similar to those of modern-day psychedelics, including hallucinations, altered perceptions, and euphoria. The plant was also believed to have therapeutic properties and was used to treat a variety of ailments.

Another possible psychedelic substance used by the ancient Egyptians is the Datura plant (*Datura Stramonium*). This plant was known as "Thorn Apple" and was used for its psychoactive properties. The plant was believed to have been used in rituals and ceremonies and may have been used by the ancient Egyptians for divination purposes. There are also references in ancient texts to a substance known as "The Tears of Horus." It is unclear what this substance was, but it is believed to have been a psychoactive substance that was used in religious rituals.

The use of psychedelics in ancient Egypt isn't well-documented. However, it is clear that the ancient Egyptians had a deep knowledge of the properties of plants and may have used them for their psychoactive effects as well as their medicinal benefits.

The use of psychedelics such as cannabis and opium in ancient China is documented in texts, such as the Tao Te Ching and the Yellow Emperor's Classic of Internal Medicine. These substances were used for their medicinal properties and were also used in religious ceremonies.

Evidence of smoking in the ancient world was found in 2019 while digging in an ancient graveyard in the Pamir Mountain range. Archaeologists found Toombs dating back to 2500 years ago that had wooden braziers filled with stone covered in Cannabinol. This is a product of the main psychoactive substance in cannabis known as Tetrahydrocannabinol (THC).

Some evidence also suggests the use of psychedelics in ancient Spain. The hair found in a Spanish burial cave revealed that humans living 3,000 years ago used hallucinogens derived from local plants as part of their rituals. Chemical analysis of the hair revealed evidence of Ephedrine, Atropine and Scopolamine substances known to produce altered states of consciousness.

Each hair strand suggested that the drugs were consumed well over a year before their death. Ephedrine is a stimulant that provides bursts of energy and mental clarity. Atropine and Scopolamine are potent deliriants that can produce hallucinations and out-of-body experiences. The presence of these drugs suggests that the people who used them were guided by someone who understood their power.

In ancient Greece, the use of psychedelics such as ergot and opium is documented in texts such as the Iliad and the Odyssey. These substances were used for their healing properties and were also used in religious ceremonies. It's believed that the Ancient Greek philosopher Plato derived his mind-matter theory from psychedelic intake. In the Eleusinian mysteries, a religious event near Athens, Plato drank a potion that some argue contained ergot, which is derived from LSD. This potion gave him heavenly visions, which he recorded in the Phaedrus.

> "They saw the blessed sight and vision and were initiated into that which is rightly called [250c] the most blessed of mysteries, which we celebrated in a state of perfection, when we were without experience of the evils which awaited us in the time to come, being permitted as initiates to the sight of perfect and simple and calm and happy apparitions, which we saw in the pure light, being ourselves pure and not entombed in this which we carry about with us and call the body, in which we are imprisoned like an oyster in its shell. So much, then, in honor of memory, on account of which I have now spoken at some length, through yearning for the joys of that other time. But beauty, [250d] as I said before, shone in brilliance among those visions; and since we came to earth we have found it shining most clearly through the clearest of our senses; for sight is the sharpest of the physical senses, though wisdom is not seen by it, for

wisdom would arouse terrible love, if such a clear image of it were granted as would come through sight, and the same is true of the other lovely realities; but beauty alone has this privilege, and therefore it is most clearly seen [250e] and loveliest." **Plato (Phaedrus, 250-c)**

Plato's description appears to encapsulate a profound and enigmatic encounter, which could potentially mirror the sensations encountered by individuals in altered states of consciousness. The term "Initiation into the Most Blessed of Mysteries" might parallel the transition from normal awareness to an expanded, transcendent realm—an altered state where consciousness is transformed. The altered state is typified by the emergence of "perfect and simple and calm and happy apparitions," signifying a departure from the mundane into a domain of amplified perception and profound insight.

The reference to "pure light" and the state of being "pure" could metaphorically embody the lucidity and transcendence often associated with psychedelic experiences. The notion of being "imprisoned like an oyster in its shell" could allegorically represent the limitations of the corporeal body and the potential liberation of the mind during altered states.

The passage's accentuation of beauty and its brilliance within the visions might be construed as a manifestation of the heightened aesthetic encounters that frequently accompany altered states. The assertion that "beauty alone has this privilege" to be distinctly perceived could imply that, in these states, the perception of beauty becomes intensified and unobstructed.

Under this interpretation, the passage resonates with the insights and encounters often recounted by Psychonauts who delved into altered states facilitated by diverse substances. Nevertheless, it is crucial to recognize that while this perspective provides an engaging framework for understanding Plato's narrative, definitive claims regarding his potential exposure to ergot or any other substance remain uncertain.

However, it is certain that Plato believed in dualism, particularly in the context of his philosophy of mind and metaphysics. Dualism, in the context of Plato's philosophy, refers to the idea that reality is composed of two distinct substances or realms: the physical/material world and the world of Forms or Ideas. Plato's dualism can be understood through his theory of the divided line and his allegory of the cave, both of which are found in his most famous work, "The Republic."

Plato presents a hierarchy of reality that consists of four levels. The lowest level is the world of physical objects, which are subject to change and imperfection. Above that is the world of visible and sensible objects, which includes things we perceive with our senses. The third level is the realm of mathematical and abstract concepts, which are more stable and unchanging than physical objects. The highest level is the realm of Forms or Ideas. According to Plato, these forms are the ultimate reality, representing the perfect and unchanging essence of things, separate from the imperfect physical world.

[Photo from: http://2.bp.blogspot.com/-f6OV-DVNv-E/T5lPqzLPrTI/
AAAAAAAACSs/jNklI6o1fio/s400/cave-2.jpg*]*

Plato uses the analogy of prisoners in a cave to illustrate his dualistic perspective. The prisoners are chained and facing a wall, and all they can see are the shadows cast on the wall by objects behind them. These shadows represent the physical world perceived through the senses. Plato suggests that the prisoners' perception of reality is limited and distorted, just like our perception of the physical world. The outside world, illuminated by the sun, represents the realm of forms, which is a higher reality that can only be grasped through reason and intellectual insight.

Plato's dualistic perspective finds its origins in his staunch belief in the immutability and eternity of the Forms. He posited that the physical realm remains in a perpetual state of flux and imperfection, contrasting sharply with the unchanging and flawless nature of the realm of Forms. According to Plato, the physical world merely reflects or imitates the superior reality embodied by the Forms, albeit in an imperfect manner. These conclusions emerged as a result of his extensive philosophical inquiries into the fundamental aspects of reality, knowledge, and the intricate interplay between material and immaterial facets of existence.

In a parallel vein, Plato's dualism presents a challenge to the prevalent notion that the material world encompasses the entirety of reality. Correspondingly, the realm of psychedelics has the capacity to rupture the confines of a materialistic worldview by facilitating encounters that transcend the boundaries of ordinary sensory perceptions. These encounters possess the potential to propel individuals into a realm of questioning concerning the very essence of reality. This, in turn, beckons the consideration of the conceivable existence of dimensions that extend beyond the confines of the material realm.

Plato's dualistic beliefs can be discerned in select Christian and Hindu traditions, as they too grapple with the interplay between the material and immaterial aspects of existence and the quest to understand the ultimate nature of reality.

PSYCHEDELICS AND RELIGION

Let's look into the connection between psychedelics and certain religions. The gnostic teaching of mushrooms refers to the belief that mushrooms, particularly psychedelic ones such as psilocybin mushrooms, contain a divine or mystical essence that can lead to spiritual awakening and enlightenment. This concept has roots in ancient gnostic traditions, which viewed the material world as a prison that trapped the soul and sought to transcend it through spiritual knowledge. According to this belief system, the consumption of certain mushrooms can allow an individual to temporarily break free from the constraints of the physical world and enter a state of heightened consciousness or gnosis. Gnosis refers to a type of knowledge that is not acquired through conventional means but rather through direct experience and intuition.

The use of mushrooms as a tool for spiritual exploration and awakening is not unique to the gnostic tradition. Many indigenous cultures throughout history have used psychedelics in their spiritual practices, including the use of psilocybin mushrooms by indigenous tribes in Mesoamerica. The gnostic teaching of mushrooms emphasizes the importance of intention and mindfulness in their use. It is believed that the experience of ingesting mushrooms should be approached with reverence and respect. A certain level of spiritual preparation is necessary to fully benefit from their effects. Critics of this belief system argue that the use of psychedelics for spiritual purposes can be dangerous and unpredictable and that there are other safer methods of achieving spiritual enlightenment. However, proponents of the gnostic teaching of mushrooms maintain that when used responsibly and with proper guidance, mushrooms can be a powerful tool for self-discovery and transformation.

If someone came to your door and said, "Excuse me sir, would you like to hear about the sacred known as Jesus Christ." You'd probably slam the door in their face and think they're some kind of hippie trying to sell you mushrooms. Believe it or not, there are many ancient historians and religious scholars who believe this theory: that the story of Jesus Christ is just an encrypted message from the psychedelic experience of mushrooms. This theory was popularized by John Marco Allegro, an ordained minister who was selected to translate the Dead Sea Scrolls. Through his 14 years of studying, he came up with the conclusion that religion is based on the concept of people tripping on mushrooms. He was able to trace back the origins of Jesus to a Sumerian translation—a mushroom covered in God's semen. God's semen was considered the rain. After it rained, mushrooms would appear. When people consumed these mushrooms, they started having psychedelic visions of God.

It is, therefore, believed that Jesus was the mushroom created from the seed of God, and only through his flesh and blood can you receive enlightenment from God. The Holy Grail was nothing but a mushroom filled with rainwater. All this was lost in translation from trying to hide this information from the Romans. Allegro stated:

> "The origins of the New Testament were devised to spread the rights of mushroom worship to the faithful. Jesus in the gospel was code for Amanita Muscaria (Fly Agaric). Christianity is nothing but a religion that involves the use of psychedelic plants as a way to access the divine mystery."

In no way am I trying to convince Christians that the Lord and Savior is a mushroom, but I do find it interesting that the Vatican cut the rights to the book, made it unavailable and destroyed Allegro's career and credibility. There are many different references to psychedelic usage in religion; you just have to know what you're searching for and how to take the interpretation.

In the book of Exodus, the Israelites become hungry; they have been in the woods for over 40 years. God gave them this bread, which is called "Mana." Mana is a derivative of the Aramaic word "Man Hu," which means "What is it?" **Exodus 16:14-29 King James Version**

> [14] " And when the dew that lay was gone up, behold, upon the face of the wilderness there lay a small round thing, as small as the hoar frost on the ground. [15] And when the children of Israel saw it, they said one to another, It is manna: for they wist not what it was. And Moses said unto them, This is the bread which the Lord hath given you to eat. [16] This is the thing which the Lord hath commanded, Gather of it every man according to his eating, anomer for every man, according to the number of your persons; take ye every man for them which are in his tents. [17] And the children of Israel did so, and gathered, some more, some less. [18] And when they did mete it with an omer, he that gathered much had nothing over, and he that gathered little had no lack; they gathered every man according to his eating. [19] And Moses said, Let no man leave of it till the morning. [20] Notwithstanding they hearkened not unto Moses; but some of them left of it until the morning, and it bred worms, and stank: and Moses was wroth with them. [21] And they gathered it every morning, every man according to his eating: and when the sun waxed hot, it melted."

Manna is also referenced in **John 6:53-57**:

> [53] Jesus said to them, "Very truly I tell you, unless you eat the flesh of the Son of Man and drink his blood, you have no life in you.

[54] Whoever eats my flesh and drinks my blood has eternal life, and I will raise them up on the last day.

[55] For my flesh is real food, and my blood is real drink.

[56] Whoever eats my flesh and drinks my blood remains in me, and I in them.

[57] Just as the living Father sent me and I live because of the Father, so the one who feeds on me will live because of me. [58] This is the bread that came down from heaven. Your ancestors ate **manna** and died, but whoever feeds on this bread will live forever."

Now, I highly doubt Yeshua was referring to cannibalism. It's also ironic that the holiday based on Yeshua's presumed birthday has mushroom symbolism planted all over it.

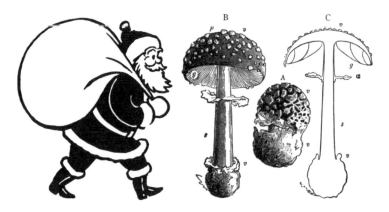

Santa is depicted in red and white, which is symbolic of the Amanita Muscaria Mushroom, which brings gifts of euphoric states of consciousness. Like gifts, they are found beneath pine trees in Siberia. The snowfall in northern Siberia during the winter is so heavy that ground-level access is nearly impossible. This is why many homes are built with roof access. Shamans had a tradition of dressing up like the red and white pattern of the Amanita Muscaria Mushroom. The shamans' holistic practices were banned, hence why they would sneak on the roof to deliver medicines and "Gifts."

They were healers and knew the power of the mushrooms and used mushrooms as medicine. Shamans traveled through the forest in sleighs that were pulled by reindeer. Reindeer are common in Siberia and Northern Europe. The male reindeer loved the Amanita Muscaria Mushroom. Biologists who studied the fungi suggest Siberian tribesmen who ingested the mushrooms may have hallucinated the grazing Reindeer that were flying. Rudolph is another example of mushroom imagery. His bright red nose looks exactly like a mushroom or a mushroom being consumed by a reindeer. The shamans would place the mushrooms on the tree and let them dry out.

They placed them in their sacks to sell to people. Mushrooms would be placed in stockings and hung near a fireplace for them to be dried out faster and consumed. Shamans would also consume reindeer urine because the reindeer bladder would filter out the toxins. Shamans weren't the only ones who knew the power of magic mushrooms.

Ancient Egyptians depicted mushrooms in many of their hieroglyphs. Mesoamerican cultures, such as the Mayan and Aztec societies, consumed mushrooms in their religious ceremonies. Aztecs refer to the mushroom as "Teonanácatl" in Nahuatl (literally "God Mushroom"— compound of the words teo(tl) (god) and nanácatl (mushroom).

The Rig Veda in Hindu belief describes the drinking of Soma to become immortal. There's even a reference to drinking urine, which, as mentioned earlier, the Siberian shamans drink the urine to bypass the toxins. The Sanskrit word for Soma means "Distill, extract, sprinkle."

In Hinduism, it is believed that the cow is representative of the divine and natural benefits and should be protected at all costs. Cows are the embodiment of soma. Mushrooms grow from cow manure. This could be the reason why many people say, "Holy cow" or "Holy shit."

PSYCHEDELIC MUSHROOM THEORY

There's a great theory that our consciousness expanded from our ancestors eating mushrooms that grew from manure. This theory was made popular from the book "Food of the gods" by renowned ethnobotanist Terence Mckenna. McKenna explores the historical and cultural significance of psychoactive plants and fungi, such as Psilocybin mushrooms, Ayahuasca, and LSD.

The book is divided into three parts. In the first part, McKenna provides a historical overview of the use of psychoactive plants and fungi in different cultures and civilizations throughout history. He argues that these substances have played an important role in shaping human consciousness and society.

The Stoned Ape Theory proposes that during the last ice age, as the glaciers receded, Africa transformed, transitioning into a greener landscape marked by forests and lush vegetation. However, as these forests started to dwindle, our early ancestors faced increased challenges in hunting for sustenance. In response, homo erectus began exploring alternative dietary options.

Amidst this dietary experimentation, a pivotal discovery was made. Homo erectus stumbled upon a type of mushroom that could be compared to the fictional "Limitless pill" depicted in the movie "Limitless." Where the protagonist experiences heightened consciousness and ascend the ranks of the financial world. In contrast, the Homo erectus' version of this transformative experience involved a mushroom that elevated them to the top of the food chain. Interestingly, these mushrooms emerged from the dung of animals.

This unexpected finding yielded remarkable benefits. Consumption of these mushrooms enhanced the homo erectus' vision, thereby improving their hunting capabilities. Additionally, their heightened sex drive positively impacted reproductive success, contributing to the survival and proliferation of the species. Over numerous generations of integrating these mushrooms into their diet, the Homo erectus brain underwent an evolutionary process that promoted creativity and innovation. This newfound creativity facilitated improved communication and the ability to convey complex ideas effectively.

It's important to note that the Stoned Ape Theory is speculative in nature, yet it holds a degree of credibility. Evidence from various cultures across different historical periods depicts mushrooms as vehicles for enlightenment, as evident in artistic representations. While the theory remains unverified, it provides a thought-provoking perspective on the potential role of psychedelic substances in shaping human evolution and cognitive development. The oldest representation of mushrooms was discovered in a cave painting in the Tin-Tazarift rock-art site in Tassili, Algeria, dating back to 4700 BCE.

Cave art in Tassili n'Ajjer SE Algeria, cica 4700 BC. On the right, you see what the artwork looks like today. On the left, a rendition by artist Kat Harrison for Food of the Gods: The Search for the Original Tree of Knowledge, of what was originally depicted.)

PHOTO CREDIT: *Institute of Archaeology RAS—Archaeologists are rushing to preserve rock images of ancient 'magic mushroom whale-hunting' people in Eurasia's most northerly art gallery at Pegtymel, Chukotka, dating to 2,000 years back* Selva Pascuala mural dating back to 6,000 years ago

The Selva Pascuala rock painting, with a bull at the upper left and mushrooms at the lower right Photo by Alan Piper

Health Benefits of Cheat Codes

When used properly, certain cheat codes have many different health benefits. We'll start with Magic Mushrooms. Magic Mushrooms contain a molecule called psilocybin. Psilocybin is a psychoactive drug that is rapidly converted in the body to a compound known as psilocin. Psilocin activates serotonin receptors in the brain. Serotonin plays a vital role in mood, sex, appetite and motivation.

The Johns Hopkins University School of Medicine has conducted extensive research on the therapeutic potential of psilocybin. The researchers report that a small number of longtime smokers who had failed many attempts to drop the habit did so after a carefully controlled and monitored use of psilocybin in the context of a cognitive behavioral therapy treatment program.

In a small double-blind study, Johns Hopkins researchers report that a substantial majority of people suffering from cancer-related anxiety or depression found considerable relief for up to six months from a single large dose of psilocybin—the active compound in hallucinogenic "Magic Mushrooms."

Six months after the final session of treatment, about 80 percent of participants continued to show clinically significant decreases in depressed mood and anxiety, with about 60 percent showing symptom remission into the normal range. 83 percent reported an increase in well-being or life satisfaction. Some 67 percent of participants reported the experience as one of the top five meaningful experiences in their lives, and about 70 percent reported the experience as one of the top five spiritually significant lifetime events. A professor of behavioral biology in the Departments of Psychiatry and Behavioral Sciences and of Neuroscience at the Johns Hopkins University School of Medicine, Roland Griffiths, Ph.D., said:

> "The most interesting and remarkable finding is that a single dose of psilocybin, which lasts four to six hours, produced enduring decreases in depression and anxiety symptoms. This may represent a fascinating new model for treating some psychiatric conditions."

He notes that traditional psychotherapy offered to people with cancer, including behavioral therapy and antidepressants—which can take weeks or even months—isn't always effective, and some drugs, such as benzodiazepines, may have addictive and other troubling side effects.

The usage of mushrooms in the context of cancer patients has gained some attention due to the potential therapeutic properties of certain mushroom species. One mushroom that has been studied extensively is the "Turkey Tail" mushroom (scientifically known as Trametes Versicolor). It contains compounds called polysaccharopeptides (PSP) and polysaccharide-K (PSK), which have been investigated for their potential anti-cancer properties.

Research has shown that these compounds may help stimulate the immune system and enhance the effectiveness of certain cancer treatments, such as chemotherapy and radiation therapy. Some studies have reported improved survival rates and quality of life in cancer patients who received PSKas an adjuvant therapy.

Another mushroom of interest is the "Reishi" mushroom (*Ganoderma Lucidum*). Reishi mushrooms contain bioactive compounds like triterpenes, polysaccharides, and ganoderic acids, which have shown potential anti-inflammatory and immune-enhancing effects. While research is still ongoing, some studies have suggested that Reishi mushroom extracts may have anti-tumor effects and can improve immune function in cancer patients.

It's important to emphasize that while mushrooms may show promise, they shouldn't be considered as a substitute for conventional cancer treatments. Instead, they may be used as complementary approaches to support overall well-being and help manage certain symptoms associated with cancer and its treatments.

Marijuana, also known as cannabis, has been used for various purposes, including recreational and medicinal. The plant contains numerous chemical compounds called cannabinoids, the most well-known being Tetrahydrocannabinol (THC) and Cannabidiol (CBD).

THC and CBD exhibit different therapeutic properties, which have led to their specific uses in medicine. THC has analgesic (pain-relieving), antiemetic (anti-nausea/vomiting), and appetite-stimulating Properties. CBD, on the other hand, has anti-inflammatory, anticonvulsant, anxiolytic (anti-anxiety), and neuroprotective properties. It is commonly used for conditions like epilepsy, anxiety disorders, and inflammation-related disorders and as a general supplement for overall wellness.

Cancer patients often experience severe pain due to the disease itself or the side effects of treatments such as chemotherapy, radiation therapy, or surgery. Some studies suggest that marijuana, particularly its Cannabinoids, can provide relief from cancer-related pain.

Both THC and CBD can cause side effects, although they differ in nature and severity. THC's psychoactive properties can lead to temporary cognitive impairment, increased heart rate, dry mouth, and potential anxiety or paranoia in high doses. CBD is generally well-tolerated, with minimal side effects reported, such as mild drowsiness, dry mouth, or changes in appetite.

It's important to note that THC and CBD often work synergistically when present together, along with other cannabinoids and compounds in the cannabis plant. This is known as the entourage effect, where the combined effect of various components may produce more significant therapeutic benefits than when isolated individually.

LSD (Lysergic Acid Diethylamide) is a powerful hallucinogenic substance that affects the serotonin receptors in the brain. While LSD is primarily known for its psychedelic effects and recreational use, there has been some research suggesting potential therapeutic benefits.

Some studies suggest that LSD may have therapeutic potential for mental health conditions such as depression, anxiety, and post-traumatic stress disorder (PTSD). It is believed that LSD can influence perception, cognition, and emotions, which may help individuals gain new perspectives and insights. There is evidence to suggest that LSD may help reduce the frequency and intensity of cluster headaches.

However, this remains an area of ongoing research. Some studies indicate that LSD-assisted therapy may be beneficial in treating substance abuse disorders, particularly alcoholism. LSD can potentially induce mystical or profound experiences, which might facilitate a shift in perspective and aid in breaking patterns of addiction. It's noted that the creator of Alcoholics Anonymous (AA), Bill Wilson, considered the use of LSD as a potential tool in the treatment of alcoholism.

Bill Wilson did have experiences with psychedelic substances, including LSD, during the 1950s and 1960s. He believed that these substances could potentially aid in providing a spiritual experience or a"Spiritual awakening" similar to the transformative experiences reported by some AA members.

However, this was a personal belief and not an official stance of Alcoholics Anonymous. LSD has been investigated to be a potential aid in addressing end-of-life anxiety and providing comfort to individuals with terminal illnesses. The substance's ability to induce profound experiences and alter perceptions may help individuals come to terms with their mortality.

It's essential to reiterate that the therapeutic potential of LSD is still being explored, and it should never be used recreationally or without proper medical supervision. LSD can produce intense psychological effects that have the potential for adverse reactions or triggering underlying mental health conditions.

MOTHER AYA

Ayahuasca is a psychoactive brew that has been used for centuries by indigenous communities in theAmazon rainforest for spiritual and medicinal purposes. The term "Ayahuasca" refers to both the brewitself and the vine (Banisteriopsis Caapi) from which it is primarily made. The brew also typicallyincludes leaves from the Psychotria Viridis plant or other plants containing the hallucinogeniccompound Dimethyltryptamine (DMT).

Ayahuasca has gained global attention in recent years as interest in plant-based medicines and psychedelic substances has grown. The brew is known for inducing profoundly altered states of consciousness characterized by vivid visions, introspection, and spiritual experiences. It is often consumed in ceremonial or ritual settings under the guidance of experienced practitioners, such as shamans or healers.

Churches in the United States are starting to incorporate Ayahuasca into their practices. The most well-known religious group incorporating Ayahuasca in the United States is the Santo Daime church. Santo Daime is a syncretic Christian religion with roots in Brazil that combines elements of indigenous shamanism, African traditions, and Christianity. The church's central sacrament is Ayahuasca, which they believe facilitates direct communication with the divine. Santo Daime churches have been established in various states across the U.S., including Oregon, New Mexico, and Hawaii.

The União do Vegetal (UDV) is another Brazilian-based religious group that uses Ayahuasca as a sacrament and has branches in the

United States. The UDV integrates Christian beliefs and indigenous traditions. They emphasize the spiritual and healing aspects of Ayahuasca ceremonies and have obtained legal protection for their religious use of the brew in the U.S. through court cases.

It's important to note that the incorporation of Ayahuasca into these religious practices has faced legal challenges and scrutiny. The courts have ruled in favor of some religious groups, recognizing their rights to use Ayahuasca as part of their religious rituals under the Religious Freedom Restoration Act(RFRA). These cases have resulted in exemptions for specific religious organizations, allowing them to continue their Ayahuasca ceremonies under certain conditions and with safeguards in place.

The effects of Ayahuasca can vary from person to person. Common experiences include visual and auditory hallucinations, emotional catharsis, heightened introspection, and a sense of connection to nature, others, and the universe.

These experiences are often described as deeply transformative and can lead to insights, personal growth, and a reevaluation of one's life and values. From a scientific perspective, Ayahuasca is believed to exert its effects through the interaction of its chemical compounds with the brain's serotonin system.

THE DMT EXPERIENCE

Now, let's dive into another powerful psychedelic compound that belongs to the Tryptamine family. Dimethyltryptamine (DMT) is a potent psychedelic compound found in various plant species and the human body. It is known for its short-acting, intense psychedelic effects, often associated with profound mystical experiences.

Chemically, DMT is structurally similar to serotonin, a neurotransmitter that plays a crucial role in regulating mood, cognition, and perception. DMT exerts its effects primarily by binding to serotonin receptors in the brain, particularly the 5-HT2A receptor.DMT has been used for centuries in shamanic and spiritual practices by indigenous cultures in the form of Ayahuasca, a brew made from plants containing DMT. In recent years, DMT has gained significant attention in the realms of neuroscience, psychology, and psychedelic research. When consumed, it can produce a rapid onset of effects, leading to a complete shift in perception and a sense of entering a different reality or dimension. Many users report encountering vivid visual hallucinations, intricate geometric patterns and encounters with seemingly autonomous entities.

Users' experience with DMT can vary. Common themes include a sense of ego dissolution, time distortion, and feelings of interconnectedness with the universe. Users often report gaining insights, experiencing spiritual revelations, and undergoing personal introspection. The effects of DMT are relatively short-lived compared to other psychedelics, typically lasting around 10–30 minutes, although the overall experience may feel much longer due to the alteration of time perception.

My personal interest in DMT came after hearing about a man who experienced a DMT trip where he had a wife and kids and lived with them for over twelve years. When he returned to his original family, he was depressed because he missed his family that he thought he had been with for the last twelve years. His DMT trip was no longer than fifteen minutes, but it made him experience a time dilation of twelve years where his consciousness could've slipped into an ultimate dimension or another reality.

For some reason, that made me think back to the Exodus and the story of Moses and the burning bush. How that too could've just been a parable of a psychedelic trip. Moses comes across a burning bush and has visions of god. God tells Moses his plan for the nation of Israel. **Exodus 3-12:**

> "⁴ When the Lord saw that he had gone over to look, God called to him from within the bush, "Moses! Moses!" And Moses said, "Here I am."
>
> ⁵ "Do not come any closer," God said. "Take off your sandals, for the place where you are standing is holy ground."
>
> ⁶ Then he said, "I am the God of your father,[a] the God of Abraham, the God of Isaac and the God of Jacob." At this, Moses hid his face, because he was afraid to look at God.
>
> ⁷ The Lord said, "I have indeed seen the misery of my people in Egypt. I have heard them crying out because of their slave drivers, and I am concerned about their suffering.
>
> ⁸ So I have come down to rescue them from the hand of the Egyptians and to bring them up out of that land into a good and spacious land, a land flowing with milk and honey—the home of the Canaanites, Hittites, Amorites, Perizzites, Hivites and Jebusites.
>
> ⁹ And now the cry of the Israelites has reached me, and I have seen the way the Egyptians are oppressing them.
>
> ¹⁰ So now, go. I am sending you to Pharaoh to bring my

people the Israelites out of Egypt. "

[11] But Moses said to God, "Who am I that I should go to Pharaoh and bring the Israelites out of Egypt?"

[12] And God said, "I will be with you. And this will be the sign to you that it is I who have sent you: When you have brought the people out of Egypt, you will worship God on this mountain."

Is it possible that this could have happened while Moses was under the influence of DMT? It is speculated that the bush that was burning was the Acacia bush. Acacia trees are found in Africa and abundantly along the Sinai Peninsula.

The percentage of DMT in Acacia tree bark can vary depending on the specific species of Acacia and the region in which it is grown. Generally, the concentration of DMT in Acacia bark can range from 0.1% to 2% or even higher in some cases. It's important to note that these percentages are rough estimates and can vary significantly. Different parts of the Acacia tree, such as the root bark, stem bark, and leaves, may contain different concentrations of DMT.

Now, with all this in mind, had the bush been burning and Moses inhaled it or intentionally smoked it? It would've currently induced a powerful, lengthy vision quest, in which he could've experienced powerful hallucinations, revelational thoughts, internal conflict and most importantly, connectivity to the divine.

Over the past few months, I have been conducting interviews with individuals who have experimented with DMT, living vicariously through their experiences, as I have yet to try DMT myself. One of my favorite interviews was with Audry and her husband, Altoveli, who shared their DMT Experience.

Initially, the interview was meant to be solely with Altoveli, but he requested to include his wife, as they had the experience together during their honeymoon. The interview showcased the powerful connection they had, which was truly admirable. What stood out the most to me was Audry's DMT experience, which occurred when she was at a crossroads in her life. She was about to make the transition from Mexico to the United States and was uncertain about her career path. Being an established musician in Mexico, she feared the unknown in her new journey. During the DMT trip, she started to sing, and the singing felt like a form of healing, bringing her soul to a state of peace. Surprisingly, she sang harmonically, a departure from her usual Spanish rap style. This moment was captured on recording and used as an intro to her latest album, which can be found on YouTube @ Audry Funk. Audry had always known that making music was her purpose in this world, and her DMT experience confirmed this belief, reassured by the ancestors' message. They told her that to reach another dimension, she needed to sing. DMT eliminated her fears and provided the answers she sought for her new journey in the US. This story serves as a reminder that we, as humans, are made in the creator's image and are meant to create and find our purpose. When we align with our purpose, our souls become happy and fulfilled, leading to a natural flow of things falling into place. It is essential to note that not everyone needs psychedelics to find their purpose; the answers already lie within us. We must discover how to tap into our inner genius and pull out those answers. The universe holds infinite wisdom, and it's up to each individual to embark on their unique journey of self-discovery and self-realization.

CHAPTER FIVE

REVELATIONAL KNOWLEDGE

AN EMT's LIFE-CHANGING EXPERIENCE

A few years ago, I had a life-changing call that altered the course of my existence forever. It occurred during my second year as an EMT in the Fire Department. At that stage in my career, the job had begun to feel monotonous, almost like factory work. Each cardiac arrest we responded to seemed to follow a predictable pattern. I don't mean to be insensitive, but I likened it to being a robot on an assembly line, working on a car. One person would initiate CPR, another would establish an IV, the paramedic would administer medications, and a crew member from the engine team would establish an airway, all while the medic in charge handled an advanced airway.

For those unfamiliar with the term, a cardiac arrest is when the heart suddenly stops beating. The lack of blood flow to the brain and other organs can lead to loss of consciousness, disability, or even death if not promptly treated. According to the National Institute of Health (NIH), 9 out of 10 people who experience a cardiac arrest outside a hospital setting often die within minutes. This is typically caused by an electrical disturbance in the heart and is different from a heart attack, which results from the blockage of a coronary artery.

The main symptom of cardiac arrest is the loss of consciousness and unresponsiveness. Clinically, the person is considered dead until a pulse is reestablished or there is a Return of Spontaneous Circulation (ROSC). Throughout most of my tenure in the fire department, I had never encountered anyone under the age of 30 suffering a cardiac arrest. However, there was one instance where my youngest patient survived, and I had the opportunity to speak with her after her near-death experience. She had been lifeless for over 15 minutes, but deep down, I had a strong feeling that we could bring her back because CPR was started immediately after her family witnessed her go unresponsive.

We performed CPR and administered a few rounds of epinephrine before finally achieving a shockable rhythm. After the first dose of electricity, we obtained a pulse and initiated our post-cardiac arrest interventions while en route to the hospital.

Upon our arrival at the hospital, we provided a report and handed over care to the hospital staff. While my partner began working on their report, I started to clean the equipment. As I packed up the medical bag, I noticed that our pulse oximetry was missing. I was certain it must still be with our patient, so I asked the nurse for permission to go back into the room and retrieve the missing Pulse ox probe.

The nurse granted me permission, and as I entered the room, I saw our patient sitting up, staring at the wall with a blank expression. She didn't acknowledge my presence in the room. I had never had the opportunity to speak to someone who had come back from the brink of death, and I felt intensely curious about what she might have experienced. Did she see God? Did she visit heaven and return?

I felt a strong urge to ask her about her experience, and so I did. However, she continued to stare into space before finally responding. She expressed her feelings, saying:

> "I'm angry that you guys brought me back. When I finally left all the pain and emotions I was trying to escape from, you guys brought me back to it. When I was gone, I felt peace and pure bliss. I felt like I was one with the universe. It's a feeling that's hard to describe; it's just something you have to experience. It was both peaceful and joyful. I saw the beginning and end of time. I saw how everything and everyone is connected and how we are all one. I realized we are more than our bodies. I am no longer afraid of death because I know it's not the end but the beginning. After realizing this, I heard a calming voice come to me and tell me it's not my time. I must return to Earth to serve a bigger purpose. Then I woke up in the back of an ambulance. It felt like a dream that I didn't want to wake up from."

Her account left me speechless, and at the time, all I could manage to say was "Wow" before going about my day. In retrospect, I wish I had been able to say more to inquire further about her experience. Unfortunately, I would never see this woman again. Her encounter had a profound, lasting impact on me and became the catalyst for my spiritual journey. To this day, I remain grateful for that encounter. It inspired me to seek more understanding about the process of life after death.

Coincidentally, a few weeks after that encounter, during my part-time job in interfacility transportation with a private ambulance company, I found myself in an extraordinary situation. I had the unique privilege of transporting two gentlemen who had both lived through near-death experiences.

It felt as though the universe had granted me this chance because it knew I was on a journey to discover more about these profound encounters. These two elderly gentlemen provided me with two different perspectives of heaven and hell.

The first gentleman described his NDE as a dream-like state, reliving the best memory of his life. He shared, "It was a never-ending dream where I was in the woods hunting with my father. It was one of the greatest memories we had together before he passed away. I believe that reliving that memory with him was my form of heaven. I was sad when he told me I had to return to my body, but at the same time, I was happy to hear him say we will see each other again."

On the other hand, the next gentleman I transported had a different perspective. He said his NDE felt like a nightmare, reliving a series of experiences over and over again. "It felt like my soul was trapped in a form of purgatory," he explained. "I was told that in order to come back, I needed to forgive everyone who had wronged me and correct the wrongs I had done. Additionally, I had to appreciate everyone who was in my life at that moment. Once I agreed to these terms, I was able to return. I woke up in the hospital with a new perspective, and I immediately told my kids that I loved them. Throughout their time growing up, I had never really expressed my love for them as I always put work before my family."

The near-death experience had a profound impact on his perspective. He realized that he had his priorities all wrong, investing time and energy in things that weren't beneficial for his health. Work-related stress had led him to make bad life choices, neglecting to take care of his body and undervaluing his time. It was the brush with death that pointed him in the right direction. He woke up surrounded by his family, who had stood by him even when he wasn't at his best. The encounter with the angel of death gave him another chance and revealed that his family was the most important thing to him during his remaining time on Earth. He expressed deep appreciation for them and vowed never to take them for granted again.

It's important to remember that everyone's near-death experience will be different. Each person goes to a place they believe they deserve. Whether it's a form of heaven or hell, it is shaped by their consciousness. Some researchers propose the idea that the brain releases DMT during Near Death Experiences. This could potentially explain the reported psychedelic experiences, such as constantly replaying memories accumulated throughout life. The actual production and release of DMT in the human brain remains unproven. The presence and functionalities of DMT are still speculative and require further research. Due to the personal and subjective nature of NDEs, it is challenging to conduct controlled scientific studies. There is still limited empirical evidence to support claims of DMT's involvement in NDEs. NDEs are a complex phenomenon influenced by various factors, including physiological, psychological, and cultural aspects.

Multiple mechanisms likely contribute to the reported experiences. Other hypotheses propose that the fragmented memories and perceptions during NDEs may arise from oxygen deprivation. These altered states of consciousness are the brain's response to stress or trauma.

NDEs often involve an expansion of consciousness beyond the limitations of the individual self. Some individuals report experiencing a panoramic life review, where they gain a comprehensive understanding of their life's events and their impact on others. This expanded perspective can provide insights into the interconnectedness and greater purpose of life and the cosmos.

Cosmic Consciousness

Cosmic Consciousness is a concept that refers to a state of heightened awareness and interconnectedness with the universe or cosmos. It is often associated with spiritual and philosophical traditions, particularly those that emphasize the unity of all things and the existence of a universal consciousness or intelligence.

The term "Cosmic Consciousness" was popularized by the American philosopher and psychologist Richard Maurice Bucke in his book

"Cosmic Consciousness: A Study in the Evolution of the Human Mind," published in 1901. Bucke described Cosmic Consciousness as a higher form of consciousness that transcends the individual ego. It allows for a direct experience of the underlying unity and interconnectedness of all things.

According to Bucke, Cosmic Consciousness is a rare and transformative experience that can occur spontaneously or be cultivated through spiritual practices such as meditation, contemplation, and self- inquiry. In this state, the individual becomes aware of a vast and expanded sense of self that transcends the limitations of the personal ego. The boundaries between the self and the external world dissolve, and there is a sense of unity and oneness with the universe.

Cosmic Consciousness is often described as a state of profound bliss, love, and peace. People who have experienced Cosmic Consciousness report a heightened sense of interconnectedness, expanded awareness, and a deep understanding of the nature of reality. They may also have a heightened sense of intuition and a greater capacity for compassion and empathy.

One man who I believe obtained Cosmic Consciousness is Dr Walter Russell. I was invited to his museum in Waynesboro, Virginia. I felt his work truly bridged the gap between science and spirituality. Walter Russell was an American polymath, artist, and philosopher who lived from 1871 to 1963. He is known for his work in various fields, including painting, sculpture, architecture, and philosophy. Walter Russell claimed to have experienced several profound states of consciousness and what he referred to as "Cosmic Consciousness" or "Grand Illuminations." According to his own accounts, these experiences occurred spontaneously and were not achieved through conventional spiritual or meditative practices. Russell described his insights and experiences as moments of heightened awareness and direct connection with the universal mind.

Russell's grand illuminations were said to have provided him with deep insights into the nature of the universe and its underlying principles. He believed that during these moments of heightened consciousness, he directly accessed the knowledge and wisdom of the cosmos. These experiences shaped his theories on the unified nature of the universe and influenced his art, writings, and teachings. Russell believed in a unified theory of the universe, which he called the "Russell Cosmogony." According to his Cosmogony, the fundamental nature of the universe is based on the principles of energy, vibration, and balance. He proposed that the universe is a dynamic, pulsating, and rhythmic entity composed of light and that everything in the universe is interconnected.

Russell proposed that the universe is fundamentally based on the interplay of two opposing forces, which he called "Electricity" and "Magnetism." According to his theory, these forces are the building blocks of all matter and energy.

The interplay between electricity and magnetism symbolized the inherent dualistic nature of existence, where opposing forces are not seen as conflicting but as complementary and necessary for the dynamic equilibrium of the cosmos.

Electricity can be viewed as a symbol of the life force or universal energy that permeates everything. It is the divine essence that animates and sustains all forms of life and matter. Russell's emphasis on the rhythmic balance of electric charges can be interpreted as the dance of divine energy within the cosmic symphony.

Russell's depiction of energy moving in spirals suggests an ever-expanding consciousness and the continuous evolution of the universe and all beings within it. It represents the eternal journey of souls seeking higher states of awareness and self-realization.

His emphasis on living in harmony with nature and recognizing the interconnectedness of all things resonates with spiritual teachings such as Taoism. Echoing the concept of oneness and the idea that every action has ripple effects throughout the fabric of existence. Embracing this interconnectedness fosters a sense of responsibility and compassion toward all life forms.

Russell's approach to bridging science and spirituality can be seen as an invitation to recognize the creative power within each individual. By aligning with the universal principles of harmony and balance, one can consciously co-create one's reality and contribute positively to the collective consciousness.

It's important to recognize that Russell's ideas have not been substantiated or widely accepted by the scientific community. His theories and concepts are considered more philosophical and metaphysical in nature rather than grounded in empirical evidence or rigorous scientific methodology. Now, even though mainstream science rejected his cosmology, they were taking notes privately.

Walter Russell wrote a letter to Albert Einstein saying, "If you're going to steal my science, at least get it right." It's noted Walter

Russell came up with the elements of the atomic bomb. Nikola Tesla warned him to hide his Cosmology from mankind because mankind wasn't ready. Walter stated during his grand illuminations that God told him he would make him one of the greatest scientists and show the world he exists through his science.

> *"When you obtain cosmic consciousness, there is nothing no worldly teacher can teach you."* **Walter Russell**

WHAT HAPPENS AFTER WE DIE?

The concept of death used to be something scary for me to contemplate, especially as a firefighter who is constantly confronted with it and has had personal brushes with it from time to time. However, as I've learned more about it, I now find myself at a kind of peace with the idea of death whenever my time comes.

I was raised in a Christian household. I grew up believing in the afterlife divided into two main destinations: Heaven and Hell. According to this belief, Heaven is a place of eternal joy and communion with God for those who have accepted Jesus Christ as their savior and lived according to Christian principles. On the other hand, Hell is perceived as a place of punishment and separation from God for those who have rejected God's salvation or lived a life of sin.

Despite my upbringing, something about this belief never quite sat right with me. It felt as if it was a form of control, dictating one's fate based on adherence to specific beliefs and principles. Religion, at its core, can be seen as a form of mythology: a collection of narratives that seek to explain the origin of the universe, the nature of humanity, and the forces that govern our lives. Religions often incorporate myths, stories, and sacred texts to convey their beliefs and values. These myths help to establish a moral framework, provide a sense of purpose, and offer comfort to believers. In this way, religion serves as a means for humans to make sense of the world and find solace in the face of uncertainties, particularly when it comes to the question of an afterlife.

The idea that there is something beyond this earthly existence, a continuation of the soul or consciousness, provides comfort and hope to individuals who may fear the finality of death. It offers the prospect of eternal life, reunion with loved ones, or the opportunity for spiritual growth. The unknown can be daunting, and religion offers a comforting explanation for what may lie beyond the veil of mortality. Think of the analogy of blind men feeling an elephant in the context of religion. This parable illustrates how individuals can perceive truth only partially based on their limited perspectives and experiences. Each religion may emphasize different aspects of spirituality, rituals, and beliefs, but they are ultimately seeking to understand the same underlying existential questions. The various interpretations of the divine or the afterlife in different religions can be seen as different attempts to comprehend the ineffable.

As human understanding has evolved over time, so have religious beliefs and mythologies. As societies encounter new challenges and acquire new knowledge, religious doctrines adapt to the changing context. We can observe this in the many iterations and sects that have emerged within religions throughout history.

Interestingly, science also plays a role in this larger picture. While some may view science and religion as opposing forces, there are philosophical and spiritual elements that can overlap. Both seek to understand the nature of reality, the cosmos, and our place within it. As scientific knowledge expands, some traditional religious explanations may be reinterpreted or refined to align with current scientific understanding.

As we continue to explore the mysteries of the universe, both through the lens of religion and the scientific method, we may find that they are not as disparate as they initially appear. In the pursuit of knowledge and understanding, perhaps we will discover that all these different perspectives are, in fact, describing different facets of the same complex reality, like pieces of a grand puzzle waiting to be assembled. Embracing this idea of unity and interconnectedness can lead to a greater appreciation for the richness of human experience and a more profound sense of compassion and tolerance for the diversity of beliefs that shape our world. Embracing this idea is what allowed me to expand my horizons when it came to learning about other religions. While exploring the history of the religion I was raised on, I came to the conclusion that the Bible is like a game of telephone where a message is whispered from one person to another. As it passes through each person, it undergoes subtle changes. Similarly, the transmission and translation of the Bible over centuries have resulted in variations and interpretations that may differ from the original texts, where the message is no longer the same as the original. Scribes and translators made conscious and sometimes unconscious decisions when copying or translating the text, which could lead to changes in meaning or emphasis. Additionally, cultural and societal changes over time have influenced how certain passages are understood and applied. One example that highlights the challenges of translation and the evolution of language is the word for "Hell." In the original Hebrew and Greek texts, several words were used to describe different concepts related to the afterlife. These words are Tartarus, Gehenna, Sheol, and Hades. Each of these words conveys distinct meanings, and translating them into a single English word, "Hell," can oversimplify their original intentions.

Tartarus was the lower two parts of the underworld where the gods locked up their enemies. It is mentioned in 2nd Peter as a place for the fallen angels or the watchers to be imprisoned.

> *"For if God didn't spare the angels who sinned, but threw them down into Tartarus and delivered them to be kept in chains of darkness until judgment."* **2 Peter 2:4**

Gehenna was originally mentioned in the book of Matthew, "But I tell you, that everyone who is angry with his brother without a cause shall be in danger of the judgment; and whoever shall say to his brother, 'Raca!' shall be in danger of the council; and whoever shall say, "You fool!' shall be in danger of the fire of Gehenna." **Matthew 5:22**

Gehenna, or the Valley of "Ge Hinnom," is an actual place in Jerusalem where they would burn their trash and serve as a place of sacrifice. Later, it became associated with a place of punishment in Jewish Apocalypticism. There were two main takes on what Gehenna meant. The Rabbinical School of Hillel stated that the souls went to Gehenna for final judgment before annihilation.

The followers of Shammai were taught that the souls would go to Gehenna to be purified by fire until they were able to ascend. Sheol is the Hebrew underworld, just like Hades is the Greek underworld. Hades is just a place where spirits went; none of these places were meant for souls to suffer. This was how it was interpreted throughout time.

After learning the origin of Hell and how it truly wasn't a place of punishment, I started looking into other religious concepts of the afterlife. In Islam, the afterlife is referred to as the Hereafter or the Akhirah. Muslims believe in the existence of Paradise (Jannah) and Hellfire (Jahannam). Paradise is a place of ultimate bliss and reward for those who have lived righteous lives according to Islamic teachings. Hellfire is a place of punishment for those who have committed evil deeds or rejected the Islamic faith.

In Judaism, the afterlife is not emphasized as much as in other religions. Traditional Jewish beliefs focus more on the importance of leading a righteous life in the present world. Some Jewish interpretations include concepts such as Gan Eden (a heavenly garden) and Gehenna (a place of purgatory or temporary punishment).

In the Abrahamic religions, you'll notice the soul and punishment seem to be a common theme, but when you look into Hinduism and Buddhism, you'll start to notice a different theme.

Hinduism encompasses diverse beliefs regarding the afterlife. According to some Hindu traditions, the soul is reborn into a new body after death (reincarnation) based on its karma (actions and deeds). The ultimate goal is to break free from the cycle of rebirth and attain Moksha, liberation from the cycle of life and death. Buddhism teaches the concept of Rebirth, where individuals are continually reborn into new existences based on their actions (karma). The goal in Buddhism is to achieve enlightenment (Nirvana) and escape Samsāra, which is the cycle of rebirth by eliminating desire and attachment. The concept of reincarnation resonated more with my soul than the idea of spending eternity in church with God or facing eternal damnation in Hell. In my opinion, both of those concepts seemed like forms of eternal punishment.

CHAPTER SIX

REINCARNATION

"As a person puts on new garments, giving up old ones, the soul similarly accepts new material bodies, giving up the old and useless ones." —**Lord Shri Krishna, Bhagavad-Gita verse 2.22**

ENERGY CANNOT BE CREATED NOR DESTROYED.

The first law of thermodynamics, also known as the law of conservation of energy, states that energy cannot be created nor destroyed in an isolated system. It can only be transformed from one form to another or transferred between different objects or systems. This law is a fundamental principle in physics and is applicable to various natural processes and phenomena. From a metaphysical standpoint, one can explore a conceptual relationship between reincarnation and the first Law of Thermodynamics, despite the distinct domains they traditionally belong to. In this perspective, consciousness or the soul could be seen as a form of energy, not limited to physical matter but existing as a metaphysical entity. Just as energy cannot be created nor destroyed in the physical realm, the metaphysical energy of consciousness may follow a similar principle. Rather than being extinguished upon death, it is believed to persist and transform, seeking new expressions and experiences.

Energy is a fundamental aspect of the universe. Energy can manifest in various forms, such as electromagnetic radiation, chemical energy, kinetic energy, and more. According to some spiritual beliefs, human beings and all living entities possess a form of energy that transcends the physical body. Consciousness refers to the state of awareness and subjective experience. It is the ability to perceive, think, and have self-awareness. Some spiritual traditions posit that consciousness is not solely a product of the brain but rather a fundamental aspect of existence itself.

The relationship between energy and consciousness can be approached in various ways, depending on the philosophical or spiritual framework being considered. Metaphysics explores fundamental questions about the nature of reality, including the nature of consciousness and its relationship to the broader universe. Here are a few perspectives.

Panpsychism is the view that consciousness is a fundamental and ubiquitous aspect of reality. According to this perspective, all entities, from subatomic particles to complex organisms, possess some level of consciousness. In the metaphysical framework of Panpsychism, energy can be seen as an expression or manifestation of consciousness itself. Energy becomes an intrinsic property of all things, and consciousness is intimately intertwined with it.

In various eastern philosophies and spiritual traditions, such as Hinduism and Buddhism, the concept of energy is central. In these traditions, energy is often referred to as "Prana," "Chi," or "Life force." It is believed to flow through the body and be responsible for vital functions and well-being. Consciousness is seen as interconnected with this energy and influenced by its quality and flow. Practices like yoga and meditation aim to balance and enhance this energy to deepen states of consciousness and spiritual awareness.

Reincarnation is the belief in the rebirth of a soul or consciousness after death. According to this belief, when a person dies, their consciousness or soul separates from the physical body and enters into a new life or body. This process of rebirth is often seen as an opportunity for spiritual growth and learning. The link between energy, consciousness, and reincarnation can be seen in the idea that consciousness, which is considered a form of energy, continues to exist beyond the physical body and undergoes a cycle of rebirth. Some spiritual philosophies propose that consciousness is not tied to a specific individual but is part of a larger universal consciousness or collective energy.

REINCARNATION IN RELIGION

Reincarnation has fascinated and intrigued humanity across cultures and time periods. It is a fundamental belief in various religions and belief systems, including Hinduism, Buddhism, Jainism, and certain sects within Sikhism.

Hinduism is one of the world's oldest religions, with roots dating back over 4,000 years. It is a complex and diverse religion with a wide range of beliefs and practices. Hinduism encompasses a vast body of scriptures, rituals, and philosophical ideas. One of the key concepts in Hinduism is reincarnation, which plays a fundamental role in shaping the religious and philosophical outlook of its followers. Reincarnation, or Samsara, is the belief that the soul (Atman) is eternal and undergoes a cycle of birth, death, and rebirth. According to Hinduism, the soul is immortal and takes on different physical bodies in each lifetime.

The nature of the new life is determined by the moral and ethical actions (Karma) performed in previous lives. Good actions lead to a better rebirth, while negative actions result in a lower or more challenging existence. The cycle of reincarnation is seen as an opportunity for the soul to learn and evolve spiritually. Hinduism teaches that the ultimate goal of the soul is to break free from the cycle of birth and death and attain liberation, known as Moksha. Moksha represents the release from the cycle of Samsara and the merging of the individual soul with the divine. Hinduism recognizes that the universe operates on the principle of cause and effect, wherein actions have consequences. This principle is reflected in the concept of karma. Karma refers to the accumulated actions, both good and bad, performed by an individual. It influences the circumstances and experiences of each life and determines the path of future rebirths. Hinduism encourages individuals to lead a virtuous life, fulfill their social and familial duties, and strive for spiritual growth to accumulate positive karma and break free from the cycle of reincarnation.

Buddhism originated in ancient India around the 5th century BCE and emerged as a reform movement within the existing religious and philosophical landscape, which Hinduism primarily dominated. Buddhism borrowed many concepts and terms from Hinduism. For example, both religions share the concepts of Karma (the law of cause and effect) and Dharma (the moral and ethical duties).

It also embraces the idea of reincarnation, but it approaches it differently. According to Buddhism, individuals are caught in the cycle of birth and death (Samsara) due to ignorance and attachment. The goal is to attain enlightenment (Nirvana) and end the cycle of rebirth.

Buddhism rejects the notion of an eternal, unchanging self (Atman). Instead, it teaches the concept of no-self (Anatta), suggesting that there is no permanent independent entity that reincarnates. It views the self as a collection of ever-changing elements. It also acknowledges the influence of karma on rebirth. However, it emphasizes that karma is not the sole factor. It recognizes other causes and conditions that contribute to rebirth, such as craving and ignorance. In Buddhism, Nirvana is the cessation of suffering and the liberation from the cycle of rebirth. It involves realizing the true nature of reality and overcoming attachment and ignorance.

Hinduism generally believes in an upward or downward progression in reincarnation based on one's Karma. Positive actions lead to a higher birth in the next life, and negative actions result in a lower birth. In comparison, Buddhism doesn't adhere to a strict linear progression. Rebirth in Buddhism is seen as a continuous process influenced by various factors. The quality of rebirth depends on one's karma, but it also considers the individual's state of mind and spiritual development.

The ancient Egyptians believed that life did not end with death, but it continued in the afterlife. They saw death as a transitional phase to a new existence. They believed that the soul, called the "Ka," would leave the body upon death and continue its journey in the afterlife.

The concept of reincarnation, known as the "Transmigration of souls," was intricately connected to the afterlife beliefs of the ancient Egyptians. They believed that after death, the soul would travel to the Hall of Ma'at, where the heart of the deceased would be weighed against the feather of Ma'at, the goddess of truth and justice.

To ensure a successful transition and a favorable afterlife, the Egyptians believed that various rituals, ceremonies, and proper burials were essential. They preserved and mummified the bodies of the deceased to maintain the physical form for the afterlife. The mummification process involved removing internal organs, treating the body with preservatives, and wrapping it in linen bandages.

PHOTOGRAPH BY BRITISH MUSEUM, SCALA, FLORENCE: Ani's soul, represented by a bird with a human head, observes as Anubis weighs Ani's heart against the feather of Ma'at, the goddess of balance and justice.

It the heart were found to be pure and balanced, indicating a righteous life, the individual would proceed to the blissful afterlife. However, if the heart was heavy with wrongdoing, it would be devoured by a creature called Ammit, and the soul would face eternal punishment.

Reincarnation played a role in the afterlife journey of the ancient Egyptians, but it was not a continuous cycle of rebirth as in some other belief systems. Instead, they believed in a process called "Eternal Return" or "Repetitive Renewal." They believed that the blessed souls would live eternally in the afterlife, experiencing a perpetual existence similar to their life on Earth, including engaging in activities they enjoyed and being reunited with their loved ones.

The belief in the afterlife and reincarnation was deeply ingrained in ancient Egyptian society and influenced many aspects of their culture, including religious rituals, burial practices, and the construction of elaborate tombs and monuments. The Egyptians aimed to secure a prosperous afterlife through their actions and devotion to the gods during their earthly lives.

SCIENTIFIC PROOF OF REINCARNATION

Scientific investigation of reincarnation is a highly controversial and debated topic within the scientific community. Many scientists are skeptical of the concept due to its lack of empirical evidence and the challenges associated with studying subjective experiences and memories.

Proponents of reincarnation research argue that there are cases that warrant further investigation. They point to certain instances where individuals, often children, have provided detailed and accurate information about people, places, and events from a historical period that they would not have otherwise been exposed to in their current lives.

Some researchers employ rigorous methodologies to investigate these claims. They typically start by gathering detailed accounts from individuals who claim to remember past lives, documenting their statements and any other available evidence. This may involve interviews, psychological evaluations, and the examination of relevant historical records.

Once the initial information is collected, researchers may attempt to verify the accuracy of the claims by comparing the reported memories with historical facts. They investigate whether the individuals could have obtained the knowledge through normal means such as books, movies, or conversations with family members. If there is no plausible explanation for the knowledge, some researchers consider the possibility that the memories could be attributed to a past life.

There have been a few well-known researchers in the field, such as Dr. Ian Stevenson and Dr. Jim B. Tucker, who have published studies and books on reincarnation research. They have documented cases of children who have reported past-life memories and have conducted investigations to verify the accuracy of their claims. Dr. Ian Stevenson was a prominent psychiatrist and researcher who dedicated a significant portion of his career to studying cases of claimed reincarnation. He conducted extensive investigations into the phenomenon and documented numerous cases from around the world. His work aimed to provide empirical evidence for the existence of past lives.

One of Dr. Stevenson's notable contributions is his collection of over 2,500 case reports of children who claimed to remember past lives. These cases were meticulously documented, including detailed interviews with the children, their families, and other individuals involved. Dr. Stevenson traveled extensively to investigate these cases firsthand, often visiting the locations the children claimed to be. Dr. Stevenson found that children who died a very traumatic death had the strongest recall of their previous life, from the names of their previous family members to the places they once lived. He thought that the intense emotional experience resulting from trauma at the moment of death was carried forward into the next life by the psyche.

He sought to rule out alternative explanations for the children's memories, such as fraud, coincidence, or Cryptomnesia (unconscious recall of forgotten information). He employed rigorous methods to verify the accuracy of the reported details by comparing them with historical records and conducting interviews with individuals who had knowledge of the deceased individuals mentioned by the children.

Dr. Stevenson's work resulted in the publication of several books, including "Twenty Cases Suggestive of Reincarnation" (1966), "Cases of the Reincarnation Type" (1975), and "Where Reincarnation and Biology Intersect" (1997). These books present detailed case studies and analysis of the evidence he collected throughout his career.

It's important to note that while Dr. Stevenson's work has received attention and sparked interest in the field, it remains controversial within the scientific community. Skeptics argue that his methods were not foolproof and that alternative explanations, such as Confabulation or Selective Memory, could account for the reported memories. Since Dr. Stevenson's time, other researchers, including Dr. Jim B. Tucker, have continued to investigate reincarnation cases and build upon his work. Dr. Tucker, a colleague and successor to Dr. Stevenson at the University of Virginia, has conducted his own research, documented additional cases, and published books such as "Life Before Life: A Scientific Investigation of Children's Memories of Previous Lives" (2005). Dr. Jim B. Tucker is a psychiatrist and researcher who carried on the research legacy of Dr. Ian Stevenson in reincarnation studies. Dr. Tucker, director of the Division of

Perceptual Studies at the University of Virginia School of Medicine, has focused his research on children who report detailed memories of past lives, often with specific information about people, places, and events that they could not have known through normal means. These cases are referred to as "Spontaneous past-life memories."

Through his investigations, Dr. Tucker has documented numerous intriguing cases of children recalling past-life memories and has published several books on the subject. His books include "Life Before Life: A Scientific Investigation of Children's Memories of Previous Lives" and "Return to Life: Extraordinary Cases of Children Who Remember Past Lives." In these works, he presents compelling evidence and detailed case studies supporting the idea of reincarnation.

Dr. Tucker employs rigorous methods in his research, including interviewing the children, their families, and other individuals connected to past-life memories. He also explores any available records, documents, and other historical information to corroborate the children's claims. His aim is to provide scientific analysis and data to better understand the phenomenon of past-life memories and their implications for our understanding of consciousness and the nature of life.

Dr. Ian Stevenson and Dr. Tucker's work on reincarnation remains a subject of debate within the scientific community. Despite the evidence presented, their work has not been accepted as conclusive proof of reincarnation.

Favorite Reincarnation Story

Growing up in a Christian household, reincarnation isn't commonly accepted as a belief. However, most of my family would never deny that it's a possibility. We would often make jokes, saying, "He's been here before," whenever we saw a child doing something remarkably advanced at a young age. Once, my son told his mother, "I remember we were cats, and after that, I chose you to be my mommy from Heaven." Now, while many people might dismiss their kids' statements as an overactive imagination, I pay close attention when I hear a child say something out of the ordinary because I believe that the child is still connected to something profound. Some of my personal favorite stories about reincarnation come from young kids. I posted a video on Tiktok about the story of Luke Ruehlman, the boy who remembered being a black woman who died in a fire in Chicago.

The video received numerous interesting comments from people who claimed their kids also remembered their past lives. The first comment that received the most likes was both sad and comforting. It was about a daughter who remembered being aborted and then came back to her mother years later. When the daughter was two years old, she emotionally ran to her mother to describe a decision her mother had made over 19 years ago. The daughter was upset about all the blood and couldn't understand why the doctors threw her away in the trash. From her perspective, she thought that all doctors were mean, unaware that it was her mother who made the decision at the time. After the daughter revealed this, the mother hugged her tightly and cried. Following that moment, the daughter never mentioned it again, nor did she remember the incident even occurring. It was as if her soul was always meant for her mother, and after 19 years, she found her way back. What's also intriguing about that story is the shadow work that was done through reincarnation. Once the mother confronted her past, both souls were able to accept it and move on.

Soul Contracts

Humans currently exist in the third density; this is known as the veil of forgetting, where our consciousness evolves before we move on to the next density. Our souls come here to learn a lesson in a 3D form. Our souls make agreements or contracts with other souls, as well as with higher spiritual beings or guides. These contracts outline the various experiences, lessons, and challenges we will encounter in our lifetime, as well as the roles and relationships we will have with other individuals.

Soul contracts are seen as opportunities for spiritual growth and learning. Suffering is the catalyst to growth. These contracts are designed to help us overcome challenges, develop virtues, and expand our consciousness. The specific lessons and experiences we encounter are tailored to our individual soul's needs and aspirations.

We actively participate in co-creating our reality. While certain aspects of our lives may be predetermined in the soul contract, we also have the freedom to make choices and shape our experiences. The interplay between our free will and the predetermined aspects of our soul contract allows for a dynamic and evolving life journey.

Soul contracts extend beyond our individual experiences and include the relationships we form with others. It is believed that we enter into agreements with certain souls to meet and interact in various ways throughout our lifetime. These relationships may be intended to facilitate mutual growth, support, or the resolution of past-life karmic patterns.

Each soul has a unique purpose or mission in this lifetime. Our soul contract helps us align with our purpose and fulfill our soul's intentions. Discovering and living in alignment with our soul's purpose can bring a sense of fulfillment and meaning to our lives.

THE SOUL WITH MANY LIVES

There are many ways to access your past life, with one of them being through the akashic records or past life regression. Past life regression refers to a technique or process that aims to access and explore the memories, experiences, or impressions of past lives that an individual may have lived before their current incarnation.

Past life regressions can be seen as a tool to tap into the reservoir of memories stored within the soul and bring them into conscious awareness. It is believed that by exploring past lives, individuals can gain insights, heal emotional or karmic patterns, understand current life challenges, and accelerate their spiritual growth.

Metaphysical practitioners, such as hypnotherapists or regression therapists, often facilitate past-life regression sessions. These sessions typically involve inducing a relaxed or altered state of consciousness. You can achieve this through hypnosis or other meditative techniques that access the subconscious mind and retrieve past life memories. Clients are guided through a series of questions or visualizations to help them recall details about their past lives and explore the associated emotions, lessons, and connections to their present lives. The memories accessed during these sessions are subjective and symbolic in nature. They may manifest as vivid images, feelings, sensations, or intuitive knowing.

Interpretation of these memories is often based on the understanding that individuals choose their life circumstances and relationships before birth to learn specific lessons or resolve unresolved issues from past lives. Dolores Cannon was a renowned hypnotherapist and author who delved into past life regression work and explored a wide range of metaphysical topics. She developed a unique approach to past life regression called the Quantum Healing Hypnosis Technique (QHHT), which aimed to help individuals access not only their past lives but also their higher consciousness or "Subconscious mind."

Cannon's past life work involved inducing a deep trance state in her clients through hypnosis, allowing them to access their subconscious mind and tap into past life memories. She believed that the subconscious mind holds vast knowledge and can provide information about past lives, soul contracts, and the purpose of one's current life.

During her sessions, Cannon's clients would often recount detailed past life experiences, including specific historical periods, places, and significant events. She encouraged clients to explore their emotions, relationships, and lessons from these past lives and to gain insights that could be applied to their present life challenges.

In addition to past life regression, Cannon's work extended beyond individual sessions. She compiled the information and insights gained from her clients into a series of books, including the "Convoluted Universe" series, which covers a wide range of metaphysical topics, including past lives, parallel realities, extraterrestrial beings, and multidimensional consciousness.

In 2022, I had my first quantum healing session with Iya Elewa, a certified reiki master and quantum healer. I am grateful to her for taking the time out of her busy schedule and flying from Detroit, Michigan, to conduct my session. To prepare for the session, she provided me with guided meditations that allowed my mind to hemi-sync.

For those of you who aren't too familiar with it, hemi-sync is a patented audio technology developed by the Monroe Institute, a research facility focused on exploring altered states of consciousness. Hemi-Sync stands for Hemispheric Synchronization and involves the use of binaural beats to create a specific pattern of brainwave activity. Binaural beats are created when two slightly different frequencies are played separately into each ear. The brain perceives the difference between the two frequencies and synchronizes its own brainwave activity to match that frequency. For example, if a frequency of 200 Hz is played into one ear and 210 Hz into the other, the brain will perceive a binaural beat of 10 Hz and begin to produce brain waves at that frequency. Hemi-sync audio recordings typically use a combination of binaural beats, soothing music, and verbal hemi-sync. By synchronizing the brain's hemispheres and guiding it into specific frequencies, individuals can enhance their mental abilities, explore altered states of consciousness, and improve their overall well-being. The effects of hemi-sync can vary from person to person, and some individuals may experience profound effects while others may notice little difference.

During my session, I vividly remembered glimpses of various past lives, ranging from a Roman gladiator to a fast-paced life in New Orleans' French Quarter as a pirate fighting against Redcoats while running a bootlegging operation. It felt like I was standing in one place, witnessing all of these lives playing out simultaneously, and the Akashic records highlighted the ones that required the most healing. The first life that stood out was when I worked as a mechanic at Amoco and tragically lost my life at the hands of my brother during a heated fight over money. I was struck in the head with a wrench, and my memory faded away after that. The Akashic records revealed an eye-opening truth: my brother in that past life is now my son in this current lifetime. When my son was born, I found myself internally blaming him for the breakdown of my relationship with his mother. Our relationship grew apart after he came into our lives. Regrettably, I didn't forge a strong bond with him and, instead, prioritized work over spending quality time with them. My obsession with making money and providing for them took precedence over being emotionally present.

He had a stronger connection with his mother, and I couldn't quite understand why we couldn't connect deeply. However, everything started to make sense as I delved into the Akashic records. It exposed my lack of accountability as a father figure and unveiled the reasons why I struggled with working with my hands. Before my session, any type of work involving power tools stressed me out, and I avoided fixing things myself, preferring to pay someone else to do it. Interestingly, my current partner Anastasia's father and brothers are all skilled mechanics great with their hands. Anastasia often expressed her joy in seeing her brothers work hard, and I envied people who were naturally gifted with their hands, like plumbers, electricians, and mechanics. Despite my desire to fix things, I constantly felt frustrated, as if something held me back.

Money served as a trigger for me, leading to issues in my past relationship with my children's mother, and it continued to affect my current relationship with Anastasia. The Akasha revealed that my connection with Anastasia is the result of a karmic debt that needs healing from a past life. In that previous life, Anastasia's essence and I had shared a life in San Francisco. I recalled this life after reflecting on a toy trolley my mother gave me as a child upon returning from a business trip to San Francisco. The trolley played the song "I Left My Heart in San Francisco."

I did leave my heart there, at least according to the vision. I remember seeing steep hills and cable cars. Although the exact time period of that lifetime remains unknown, my guess is that it was around the 1920s, judging by the fashion and the need to secretly consume alcohol, as it was prohibited during that era.

In that past life, I drank myself to death because of a tragic incident involving Anastasia. She accidentally killed our son while they were sleeping; he suffocated when she rolled over him. I was at work when this happened, and I couldn't forgive her, feeling that she should have been more careful. Our relationship grew distant, and I turned to alcohol as a means to cope, eventually drinking myself to death.

According to the Akashic Records , our deceased son reincarnated into my current grandfather, who was born in 1937, and that revelation made sense. I have always shared a very close relationship with my grandfather, often playfully claiming that I am his favorite. He has always showered us with love and care every time we visited him.

Through my quantum healing session, I realized that my son, Jevon, and Anastasia, came back into my life to provide an opportunity for forgiveness. I was advised to show them unconditional love and to recognize that the past is behind us, urging me to let bygones be bygones to break the karmic debt. The session revealed that the universe has attempted to heal me vicariously by presenting recurring themes from my past, such as Anastasia's brothers, who exemplify nothing but love for one another as mechanics.

Love conquers all, and this lesson began to sink in deeply. I was not one to cry, but after the session, the floodgates of emotion opened. I understood that addressing the traumas of my past was crucial to prevent them from manifesting in my present. My heart felt relieved as I let go of all the unhealed trauma from my past. It was as light as a feather, no longer burdened by any emotional weight. My quantum healing session taught me that everyone and everything in my life is part of the divine plan. I am meant to love and cherish everyone who comes into my life because they all play their part. I was also reminded that true wealth resides within me, and money is insignificant in the grand scheme of things.

After the session, my body felt like it had been through the wringer, leaving me physically and mentally drained. However, I couldn't help but feel curious about the time period of my previous incarnation. The last place I remembered was an Amoco repair shop. Amoco was founded on December 6, 1910, as the Standard Oil Company (Indiana) following the dissolution of John D. Rockefeller's Standard Oil Trust by the U.S. Supreme Court. The company emerged as one of the successor companies of Standard Oil, focusing primarily on the exploration, production, refining, and marketing of petroleum products. It grew rapidly in the early 20th century, becoming a major player in the U.S. oil industry. In 1985, the company changed its name to Amoco Corporation, aiming to maintain a distinct identity while still acknowledging its history as a standard oil subsidiary.

If I were to date the timeframe of my previous life, I would say it was short, spanning from the late 50s to the mid-80s, placing me in my 30s during that time. This would explain my love for music from the 70s and 80s, as listening to Hall & Oates or classic rock satisfies my soul. Whenever I work on tasks involving my hands, I always listen to classic rock or Yacht rock radio, as it helps me flow with the work at hand.

People often told me I had an old soul, and now it makes perfect sense. I have lived many lives, and the ones that needed healing were the ones the Akashic records wanted to show me. A few weeks after the session, I applied for a part-time maintenance position at the campground where I reside. Initially, I felt uncomfortable and avoided significant tasks due to a lack of confidence in my abilities. Fast forward almost a year of working there, I have learned how to handle plumbing and electrical work. I no longer shy away from tasks and take pride in fixing things. Money is no longer an issue for me as I have developed an abundance mindset towards attracting money. Most importantly, I have learned to become a better father. I am truly grateful for my session with Iya because it healed me in so many ways.

TRIGGERS FROM THE PAST

When it comes to reincarnation, I like to think of it as if your body is a car that your soul is leasing. The soul is the eternal, spiritual essence of an individual that transcends any single lifetime. It is the driving force behind each incarnation, just as the car owner is the one who initiates the lease. The car represents the physical body, which serves as the temporary vessel for the soul during one specific lifetime. Just as a leased car is used for a limited period, the physical body is utilized by the soul to experience and learn during a particular lifetime.

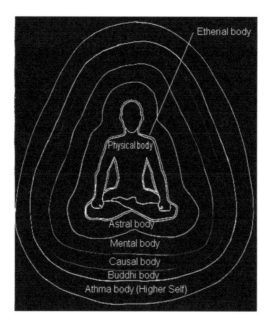

The memories of past lives are stored in the etheric bodies. The etheric body is a subtle energy body that interpenetrates the physical body. It is considered to be the template or blueprint for the physical form and contains information from past experiences.

In the car lease analogy, this could be likened to the maintenance records and history of the vehicle, which hold information about its past usage. This information is stored in the Akashic records, which your soul has access to at all times. Karma is the concept of cause and effect, where the actions and intentions from one lifetime influence future lifetimes. Similarly, the car lease analogy can be related to how the car's usage and condition during one lease period might affect the next lease agreement. Traumatic experiences in a person's life, whether physical, emotional, or psychological, can leave a profound impact on the etheric bodies. These imprints can serve as gateways to remembering past lives, as they might influence certain patterns and behaviors in current and future lifetimes.

Each individual possesses an eternal and immortal soul. This soul carries the accumulated experiences, lessons, and knowledge acquired from all past lives. Upon being reborn into a new life, the soul passes through the "Veil of forgetfulness." This veil serves a purpose as it allows the individual to focus on the lessons and experiences of their current life without being burdened or influenced by the memories of past lives. Before those memories fade away, children often recall their previous lives with greater clarity.

Even in our adulthood, we are still reminded in subtle ways. Some people remember their past lives and don't even realize they are remembering past traumas. They have unexplainable fears, with no clear understanding of their roots. These could include fear of heights, flying in planes, water, boats and even fire. For me, my triggers were money, alcohol and kids. Certain events, places, people, or experiences can act as triggers, potentially lifting the veil of forgetfulness.

This is why shadow work is very important because it removes trauma from this life and past life. The themes that keep recurring in your life are nudges from your higher self telling you that there are parts of your past that need to be healed. Some people have recurring dreams at the same place, while others can visit a city and instantly be drawn to it. Trusting your intuition and inner knowing can lead to spontaneous insights about past lives. Pay attention to strong emotional reactions or feelings of familiarity in certain situations or places.

Personally, New Orleans holds a special place in my heart; something in my soul knew I had been there before. In 2020, I embarked on a solo trip to New Orleans during Mardi Gras, and it turned out to be the best trip I had ever taken. However, it wasn't solely because of the lively partying each night but rather because my soul instantly felt at home there. The old historic architecture of the French Quarter seemed to carry a familiar energy that deeply resonated with my being. I found contentment in simply sitting on a curb, gazing at the enchanting buildings around me. The experience triggered a surge of energy and sent chills up my spine, especially when I unexpectedly came across Lafitte Blacksmith Shop Bar while on a historical ghost tour.

The Lafitte Blacksmith Shop Bar is a historic and iconic establishment located in the French Quarter of New Orleans, Louisiana. It is considered one of the oldest bars in the city. Shop Bar is believed to have been constructed sometime between 1722 and 1732, making it one of the oldest surviving structures in the French Quarter. The bar's name, "Blacksmith Shop," comes from a legend that suggests the building operated as a cover for pirate activities during the early 19th century.

The bar's namesake, Jean Lafitte, was a notorious privateer and pirate who operated in the Gulf of Mexico and the Caribbean during the early 1800s. It is said that he and his brother Pierre Lafitte used the blacksmith shop as a front for their smuggling and privateering operations. The bar's location near the Mississippi River and its secretive nature made it an ideal place for covert activities.

What's even more interesting is that during the War of 1812, Jean Lafitte and his men became known for their assistance to General Andrew Jackson during the Battle of New Orleans in 1815. Lafitte's pirates fought alongside American forces, and their expertise and bravery played a significant role in the American victory against the British. This action earned Lafitte a pardon for his past crimes from President James Madison, and he was allowed to live as a private citizen in the United States. Jean and his brother Pierre's lives were eerily similar to the life I saw in my vision. The Akasha didn't permit me to fully explore the details of this life. I'm not entirely certain whether I was one of the brothers or an associate, but I do intuitively feel that New Orleans was once a place I called home.

CHAPTER SEVEN

THE AKASHIC RECORDS

THE COSMIC LIBRARY

The term "Akasha" comes from Sanskrit and roughly translates to "Ether" or "Space." It refers to a supposed universal field of energy or consciousness that permeates the entire cosmos. According to this belief, the Akasha is an ethereal substance or dimension that exists beyond the physical realm and is accessible to those with the right spiritual insight or ability.

The akashic records are often described as a vast cosmic library or database that contains information about every event, thought, emotion, and experience that has ever occurred in the universe. It is believed that this information is imprinted or recorded in the Akasha and can be accessed by individuals through various means, such as meditation, astral projection, or deep states of consciousness.

Proponents of the Akasha suggest that tapping into the Akashic records can provide individuals with access to profound wisdom, insight into past lives, and a deeper understanding of the interconnectedness of all things. It is believed that the Akasha holds the collective consciousness of humanity and can reveal information that can help in personal growth, healing, and spiritual development.

FIGURES WHO TAPPED IN

Thoth, the Egyptian deity, and Nārada Rishi, a revered figure in Hindu mythology, are believed to have tapped into the vast expanse of the Akashic Records to acquire profound wisdom and insights. Thoth, often depicted as the ibis-headed god of wisdom and writing, is associated with the ancient Egyptian civilization. According to myth, he was the keeper of knowledge and the divine scribe. Thoth's ability to access the Akashic records is attributed to his deep understanding of the spiritual realms and his harmonious alignment with the cosmic forces.

Through meditation, ritualistic practices, and profound spiritual attunement, Thoth was able to enter a state of heightened consciousness, allowing him to navigate the ethereal dimensions and retrieve knowledge from the Akashic records. Similarly, In Hindu mythology and scriptures like the Puranas and the Mahabharata, the acquisition of knowledge by the Nārada Muni (also known as Nārada or Nārada Rishi) is described in several narratives.

According to the Puranas, Nārada Muni acquired his knowledge through his unwavering dedication to meditation, mantra recitation, and self-discipline. Nārada cultivated a deep connection with the cosmic energies. He is known to have conversations with gods, demigods, sages, and various celestial beings. Through these interactions, Nārada gained insights into different aspects of life, philosophy, and spirituality.

Nārada Muni is believed to possess the ability to remember his past lives and experiences. This divine gift of remembrance allows him to accumulate knowledge and wisdom over countless lifetimes, which contributes to his deep understanding of the universe and its workings. One can easily come to the conclusion that both Thoth and Nārada gained their insight from the Akashic records.

We must also remember Thoth and Nārada Rishi are revered figures in mythology, and their existence is primarily within the realm of mythology and folklore. They are not considered historical or factual figures; however, it is worth noting that mythology often incorporates elements and symbolism from real historical events, figures, or cultural beliefs. Some of the greatest minds of the world and psychics were known to tap into higher realms to receive visions, inspiration, and creativity.

Albert Einstein was notorious for his thought experiments. Thought experiments are mental exercises or hypothetical scenarios that scientists and philosophers use to explore or explain complex concepts. Einstein used these thought experiments extensively throughout his career to develop and test his theories, particularly in the field of theoretical physics.

One of Einstein's most famous thought experiments is the "Einstein's Elevator" experiment, which he used to explain the principles of general relativity. In this experiment, he imagined an elevator in free fall, where the effects of gravity are indistinguishable from those of uniform acceleration. By considering the experiences of a person inside the elevator, Einstein was able to illustrate how gravity affects the perception of time and space.

Another well-known thought experiment by Einstein is the "Twin Paradox." In this scenario, he imagined two twins, one of whom remains on Earth while the other travels into space at a high velocity.

According to the theory of relativity, time would pass differently for the traveling twin compared to the stationary twin due to the effects of time dilation. This experiment helped Einstein illustrate the concept of time dilation and the relativistic nature of time.

These thought experiments were crucial for Einstein's development of groundbreaking theories like the theory of relativity. They allowed him to explore the consequences of his ideas and challenge conventional wisdom. Einstein's thought experiments continue to be studied and discussed today, demonstrating the power of imaginative thinking in scientific inquiry.

Srinivasa Ramanujan, one of the greatest mathematicians of the early 19th century, developed a formula that would be used to describe black holes. This was before anyone knew what black holes were. His work became relevant in other avenues that didn't exist when he was alive, such as computer science and electrical engineering. Ramanujan often credited his mathematical abilities to a higher power or what he called his "Ishta Devata" (personal deity). Ramanujan firmly believed that his mathematical insights and discoveries were divinely inspired.

Throughout his life, Ramanujan expressed a strong spiritual and religious inclination. He believed that his mathematical talent was a gift from the Hindu goddess Namagiri. Ramanujan often attributed his mathematical ideas and formulas to dreams and visions that he believed were communicated to him by the goddess. Ramanujan dreamed of blood drops, which symbolized his goddess and how—after the dreams—he would receive visions of complex mathematical formulas unfolding.

In a letter to mathematician G.H. Hardy, Ramanujan wrote, "An equation for me has no meaning unless it represents a thought of God." He saw mathematics as a way to explore the intricacies and mysteries of the universe and considered his work a spiritual pursuit.

Ramanujan's faith and belief in the divine origins of his mathematical genius were deeply ingrained in his personality. While some of his mathematical insights were indeed groundbreaking and years ahead of his time, it's important to note that his work was also rigorously tested and verified by esteemed mathematicians. Ramanujan's contributions to number theory, continued fractions, and other areas of mathematics remain highly influential to this day.

Edgar Cayce was an American mystic and psychic. He was often referred to as the "Sleeping Prophet" because he would enter a self-induced trance-like state and provide psychic readings while asleep. Cayce's readings covered a wide range of topics, including health, spirituality, reincarnation, Atlantis, and future events.

Cayce's readings were highly regarded for their accuracy and depth of information. He provided insights into various health issues and recommended natural remedies and treatments, earning him a reputation as a pioneer in holistic medicine. Many people sought his guidance for personal and spiritual matters, and he offered insights into past lives and spiritual growth.

During his trance-like state, Cayce claimed to have access to the Akashic records and would provide detailed information about an individual's past lives, as well as insights into their current life situation, along with potential future outcomes. He believed that accessing these records could provide valuable guidance and understanding for personal growth and spiritual development.

> "Upon time and space is written the thoughts, the deeds, the activities of an entity – as in relationships to its environs, its hereditary influence; as is directed – or judgement drawn by or according to what the entity's ideal is.

Hence, as it has been oft called, the record is God's book of remembrance, and each entity, each soul – as the activities of a single day of an entity in the material world – either makes same good or bad or

indifferent, depending upon the entity's application of self towards that which is the ideal manner for the use of time, opportunity and the Expression of that for which each soul enters material manifestation.

The interpretation then as drawn here is with the desire and hope that, in opening this for the entity, the experience may be one of helpfulness and hopefulness."

— Edgar Cayce, Akashic Record Reader, in Reading 1650-1

Baba Vanga, born Vangelia Pandeva Dimitrova in 1911, was a Bulgarian mystic and renowned psychic who gained worldwide recognition for her prophecies and visions. Her extraordinary abilities began to merge after she lost her eyesight at the age of 12 due to a massive storm. According to her, the blindness acted as a catalyst for her psychic powers to develop.

Despite her visual impairment, Baba Vanga claimed that she could see into the future and communicate with spiritual beings. People from all walks of life sought her advice and guidance, including politicians, scientists, and ordinary individuals seeking answers to their most pressing questions. Over the years, her accuracy in predicting future events earned her a reputation as the "Nostradamus of the Balkans."

Baba Vanga's visions covered a wide range of topics, including natural disasters, political upheavals, and global events. She foresaw the rise and fall of political leaders, the disintegration of the Soviet Union, the Chornobyl disaster, and even the terrorist attacks on September 11, 2001. Her followers believed that her insights were divinely inspired and marveled at her ability to provide detailed information about future occurrences. Baba Vanga claimed that she could see a person's whole life in its entirety, from birth to death, as if she were watching a movie with her mind's eye.

Another person who was known to have connected to the Akashic field was **Michel de Nostredame,** commonly referred to as Nostradamus. He published a collection of prophecies called "Les Propheties" in 1555, which gained significant attention due to their cryptic and enigmatic nature.

Nostradamus' prophecies were written in the form of quatrains, which are four-line verses. They covered a wide range of topics, including wars, natural disasters, political events, and the fates of various individuals and nations. Nostradamus claimed that his predictions were based on his astrological observations and visions.

Many people believe that Nostradamus accurately predicted several historical events, such as the great fire of London in 1666, the French Revolution, the rise of Adolf Hitler, the assassinations of John F. Kennedy and Robert Kennedy, and the 9/11 terrorist attacks. However, the accuracy of these interpretations is a subject of debate and skepticism.

Nostradamus claimed that his prophecies were the result of his astrological observations and visions. He believed that celestial movements and configurations influenced human affairs and that he could tap into these influences to foresee future events.

Nostradamus was trained as a physician and had a deep knowledge of astrology, which was widely practiced during his time. Astrology was considered a legitimate science at that time and was often used to make predictions and understand the connections between celestial bodies and earthly events.

Nostradamus combined his medical and astrological knowledge with his own intuitive abilities to interpret the celestial signs and receive visions of the future. He claimed that he would enter a trance-like state and receive divine inspiration, which allowed him to perceive and understand the hidden meanings behind the celestial patterns.

According to Nostradamus, his prophecies came to him in a series of visions or dreams. He would then write down these visions in cryptic and symbolic language using quatrains, which were four-line verses to convey his predictions. Nostradamus intentionally wrote his prophecies in a vague and obscure manner, often using metaphorical language, to protect himself from potential persecution or backlash for his predictions. Critics argue that Nostradamus' quatrains are highly ambiguous and open to multiple interpretations, allowing people to find connections between his writings and historical events after they occur. They claim that the prophecies are so vague that they can be applied to a wide range of situations, and any apparent accuracy is coincidental.

IS THERE PROOF OF AN AKASHIC FIELD?

Dr. Ervin Laszlo has made significant contributions to the exploration of the Quantum Field and its implications for our understanding of reality. He has been a proponent of the idea that the quantum field is a fundamental aspect of the universe, underlying and connecting all physical phenomena.

Laszlo views the quantum field as a dynamic and information-rich medium that pervades all of space and time. He suggests that it is not simply a backdrop against which particles and forces act but rather an active and participatory element in the unfolding of reality. According to Laszlo, the quantum field is not confined to the realm of subatomic particles but extends into the macroscopic world, influencing the behavior of all physical systems.

One of the key aspects of Laszlo's work is his exploration of the relationship between the quantum field and consciousness. He proposes that consciousness is not solely a product of brain activity but is connected to the quantum field, which he refers to as the "Quantum Vacuum." Laszlo suggests that consciousness emerges from the interaction between the quantum vacuum and the neural processes in our brains and that it has a non-local and interconnected nature.

Laszlo argues that the quantum field contains a kind of cosmic memory or information storage, similar to the concept of the Akashic Records. He suggests that this informational aspect of the quantum field allows for the transmission and retrieval of knowledge and experiences beyond the limitations of space and time.

Dr. Laszlo has explored the idea of the Akashic Records from a scientific perspective. He suggests that the akashic records could be related to the quantum field, which is the fundamental energy and information field that underlies all physical reality. According to Laszlo, "The quantum field is a dynamic and interconnected web of energy and information, and it contains the blueprint for the unfolding of the universe."

Laszlo's work on the Akashic Records and the quantum field proposes that consciousness and information are fundamental aspects of the cosmos. He argues that the Akashic Records are not limited to individual experiences but also encompass collective consciousness, making them a potential source of wisdom and insight for humanity.

Dr. Laszlo's ideas are thought-provoking and have gained interest among some researchers; however, they remain speculative and are not yet widely accepted within the mainstream scientific community. The relationship between consciousness and the quantum field is a topic of ongoing exploration and debate. Further scientific evidence and investigation are needed to substantiate these ideas.

His work on the quantum field offers an interdisciplinary perspective that bridges scientific, philosophical, and spiritual concepts. It encourages us to consider the profound interconnectedness of the universe and the potential role of consciousness in shaping our understanding of reality.

The concept of quantum waves and their relationship to the Akashic records can be explored through the interplay of consciousness and the fabric of reality. In the realm of quantum physics, particles and waves exist in a state of superposition, where they can exist in multiple states simultaneously until observed or measured. This superposition is described by a wave function, which represents the probability distribution of the particle's properties. When an observation or measurement is made, the wave function collapses, and the particle manifests in a specific state.

One can easily draw parallels between this collapse of the wave function and the process of accessing the Akashic Records. The wave function can be seen as a metaphor for the interconnectedness of all consciousness and information in the universe. In this view, the Akashic Records represent a cosmic wave function that contains the infinite potential and possibilities of existence.

Just as the act of observation collapses the quantum wave function, the act of focused intention, meditation, or deep connection with one's consciousness may serve as the catalyst for accessing the Akashic records.

By attuning one's consciousness to a certain frequency or state of awareness, individuals can tap into this universal wave function and retrieve information, insights, and experiences from the collective consciousness. The Akashic Records can be seen as a realm where the waves of consciousness intersect with the waves of quantum reality.

It is within this intersection that the information and wisdom of the past, present, and even potential future events can be accessed. It is a realm where the boundaries of time and space blur, allowing individuals to gain insights beyond their immediate experience and tap into the vast tapestry of universal knowledge.

Maybe this is what Tesla meant when he stated, "My brain is only a receiver. In the Universe, there is a core from which we obtain knowledge, strength, and inspiration. I have not penetrated into the secrets of this core, but I know that it exists."

GOVERNMENT INTEREST

Several years back, I stumbled upon a 29-page document from the Central Intelligence Agency (CIA) entitled "Analysis and Assessment of the Gateway Process." Upon reading this document, I couldn't help but perceive a significant government interest in the Akashic field.

The concept of the CIA attempting to access the Akashic Records through research conducted at the Monroe Institute raises intriguing possibilities. The Monroe Institute, known for its exploration of consciousness and out-of-body experiences, has long been at the forefront of research into altered states of consciousness.

The CIA has historically displayed an interest in unconventional methods of gathering information. While primarily focused on more traditional forms of intelligence gathering, it is not surprising to consider that the CIA may have also explored the possibilities of utilizing metaphysical avenues for acquiring knowledge. In this case, their interest in the Akashic Records aligns with their pursuit of information that could potentially provide a strategic advantage.

Reaching the Akashic Records requires a deep level of spiritual attunement, profound meditation, and a state of heightened consciousness. These transcendental states are typically achieved through rigorous training, dedicated practice, and a profound connection to one's spiritual essence.

The Monroe Institute's research and methodologies may have offered the CIA a shortcut and a potential avenue for exploring altered states of consciousness, including those conducive to accessing the Akashic Records.

Techniques such as binaural beats, hemispheric synchronization, and guided imagery, developed by the institute, are believed to facilitate altered states and could have been of interest to the CIA for their potential in gathering unconventional information. The combination of binaural beats and deep meditation was how I was able to see into the records. It is no surprise that the government would take interest in this.

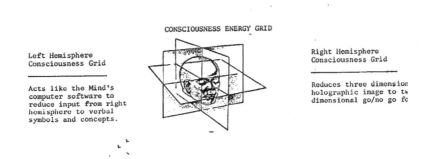

CONSCIOUSNESS ENERGY GRID

Left Hemisphere
Consciousness Grid

Acts like the Mind's
computer software to
reduce input from right
hemisphere to verbal
symbols and concepts.

Right Hemisphere
Consciousness Grid

Reduces three dimension
holographic image to tw
dimensional go/no go fo

Image from https://www.cia.gov/readingroom/docs/CIA-RDP96-00788R001700210016-5.pdf

The gateway experience is a training system designed to bring enhanced strength, focus and coherence to the amplitude and frequency of brainwave output between the left and right hemispheres. The goal was to alter consciousness, moving it outside the physical sphere to escape the restrictions of time and space.

The participant would gain access to the various levels of intuitive knowledge that the universe offers. This is different from the typical meditation because of the use of the hemi sync technique. Monroe Institute trainer Melissa Jaeger defines it as "A state of consciousness defined when the EEG patterns of both hemispheres are simultaneously equal in amplitude and frequency."

This frees the pineal gland to receive light and information from the universe or, in simple terms, see from the mind's eye. The Monroe Institute created audio techniques that can induce and sustain Hemi sync. Studies conducted by Elmer and Alyce Green at the Menninger Foundation have shown that a subject with 20 years of training in Zen meditation could consistently establish hemi-sync at will, sustaining it for over 15 minutes.

The gateway process was designed to rapidly induce a state of profound calm within the nervous system and to significantly lower blood pressure to cause the circulatory system, skeleton and all other physical organ systems to begin vibrating coherently at approximately 7-7.5 cycles per second. The resulting resonance sets up a regular repetitive sound wave that propagates in consonance with the electromagnetic field of the earth. In addition to resonating with the earth's electromagnetic sphere, the human body creates a surprisingly powerful carrier wave to assist in communication activity with other human minds similarly tuned.

After one is exposed for the first time to hemi-sync sound frequencies, they're encouraged to focus on and develop a perception and appreciation for those feelings that accompany the synchronization of the brain waves that result. Next comes the technique of progressive and systematic physical relaxation, while the hemi-sync frequencies are expanded to include additional forms of pink and white noise designed to bring the physical body to the virtual threshold of sleep. This process also aims to calm the left hemisphere of the mind while elevating the right hemisphere to a state of heightened attentiveness. Once all of this is achieved, the participant is invited to envisage the creation of an "Energy balloon" consisting of an energy flow beginning at the center of the top of the head and extending down in all directions to the feet. The energy balloon enhances the flow of bodily energy and encourages the early achievement of a suitable resonant state. It is also designed to provide protection against conscious entities possessing lower energy levels, which the participant might encounter in the event that they achieve an out-of-body state. It serves as a precautionary purpose in the unlikely event that the participant's first out-of-body experience involves direct projection outside the terrestrial sphere.

The CIA was also interested in exploring remote viewing, the psychic phenomenon that allows individuals to perceive distant or hidden locations through extrasensory perception (ESP). The CIA allegedly sought to weaponize this ability, envisioning an army of psychic spies capable of traversing boundaries and penetrating the secrets of any adversary. Intrigued by the potential applications of remote viewing in espionage, the CIA initiated a top-secret program known as Project Stargate, where they attempted to harness and weaponize this psychic ability.

Project Stargate, established in the 1970s, aimed to investigate the validity and practicality of remote viewing as an intelligence-gathering tool. The program was built upon earlier research conducted by scientists and psychical researchers, including the work of Ingo Swann, a renowned remote viewer. The CIA believed that remote viewing could potentially provide a means to access classified information that was otherwise unobtainable through conventional means.

Under Project Stargate, a select group of individuals with claimed psychic abilities were recruited and trained in the art of remote viewing. These individuals, often referred to as "Remote viewers," underwent rigorous training exercises to enhance their psychic skills. The program included various protocols and techniques to improve focus, concentration, and the ability to describe remote locations in detail.

The CIA conducted numerous experiments and operational missions using remote viewing techniques. Remote viewers were tasked with attempting to gather intelligence on specific targets, such as military installations, secret research facilities, and even the activities of foreign leaders. They were instructed to focus their psychic abilities on specific geographic coordinates or visual cues related to the targets. While the results of the remote viewing experiments varied, some instances showed intriguing outcomes. Remote viewers claimed to have accurately described remote locations, sometimes providing details that would have been impossible to obtain through conventional means. The CIA's remote viewing program was shrouded in secrecy, but in the mid-1990s, the veil of secrecy surrounding Project Stargate began to unravel.

One pivotal event that contributed to the public's awareness of Project Stargate was the release of declassified documents under the Freedom of Information Act (FOIA). These documents revealed the existence of a remote viewing program within the CIA and the Defense Intelligence Agency (DIA). They outlined the program's goals, methodologies, and some of its participants.

Additionally, a series of investigative reports and documentaries, such as the 1995 documentary "The Stargate Conspiracy" by Lynn Buchanan and the 1997 book "The Men Who Stare at Goats" by Jon Ronson, delved into the world of government-sponsored psychic research, including Project Stargate. These works further popularized and brought attention to the program.

Former participants and insiders, including remote viewers such as Ingo Swann and Joseph McMoneagle, began to share their experiences and knowledge publicly, confirming the existence of Project Stargate and providing insights into its workings. The combined efforts of researchers, journalists, declassified documents, insider testimonies, and popular media coverage gradually exposed Project Stargate to the public. This led to widespread interest, discussions, and debates regarding the ethics, effectiveness, and scientific validity of remote viewing and psychic phenomena as a whole.

It's the public shedding light on once top-secret programs like Project Stargate and analysis and assessment of the Gateway process that open doors to discussions about the potential of psychic abilities along with refueling the imaginations of those who believe in the untapped potential of the human mind and the hidden mysteries of the universe.

HOW TO ACCESS THE RECORDS

Accessing the Akashic Records is a subjective and personal experience, and it is open to individuals who are spiritually inclined and interested in exploring this realm of consciousness. It is always advisable for individuals, especially those who are young, to have a solid foundation in their spiritual development and discernment skills before engaging in any metaphysical practices. It can be beneficial to have a certain level of maturity, critical thinking, and emotional stability to navigate the profound insights and information that can be accessed through the Akashic Records.

Suppose you are considering exploring the Akashic Records or any metaphysical practice, and you are under the age of 18. In that case, it may be helpful to seek guidance and support from a trusted adult or mentor who can provide proper guidance and help you understand the potential implications and responsibilities associated with such practices. While there are various approaches and techniques to access the Akashic Records, the following is a detailed explanation based on metaphysical principles:

Invocation and sacred space:

Create a sacred space by invoking the presence of the Akashic Records and any spiritual beings or guides you resonate with. You can use prayers, affirmations, or invocations to call upon the Records and request their assistance in accessing the information you seek. Affirm your intention to access the Records and express gratitude for the opportunity.

Linda Howe is a renowned author and teacher who has popularized a specific method for accessing the Akashic Records known as the Pathway Prayer Process. Here are some of the steps based on Linda. Howe's approach: Find a quiet and comfortable space where you won't be disturbed. Set a clear intention to access the Akashic Records and create a sacred atmosphere using candles, incense, or other objects that hold personal significance.

Open with a Prayer:

Begin by opening with a specific prayer known as the Pathway Prayer. Here's an example: "I ask the akashic records to open, and I ask for the information and guidance that will be of the highest good for me at this time. I ask for protection, clarity, and insight. I am now accessing the Akashic Records."

Feel free to modify the prayer to fit your personal beliefs and language. State your full legal name aloud, including your first, middle, and last name. This helps establish a clear connection to your unique, energetic signature. Once you've stated your name, you can ask specific questions or seek guidance on a particular topic. Be clear, concise, and focused in your inquiries and intentions. It's recommended to start with general questions before moving into more personal or specific areas.

After asking your questions, take a moment to be receptive and observe any impressions, thoughts, feelings, or images that come to you. Trust your intuition and allow the information to flow. Keep a journal nearby to document your experience. Write down any insights, guidance, or messages you receive, as well as any feelings or sensations you experience during the process. When you are ready to conclude your session, offer gratitude for the insights and guidance received. You can close with a simple prayer or statement such as, "Thank you, Akashic Records, for your wisdom and guidance. I now close this session with gratitude."

Linda Howe has written books on the Akashic Records, including "How to Read the Akashic Records" and "Healing Through the Akashic Records," which provide further guidance and insights into her specific method. Remember that the Pathway Prayer Process is just one approach to accessing the Akashic Records. It is always important to find the method that resonates best with you.

Preparation and intent:

It's essential to prepare oneself mentally, emotionally, and spiritually. Set a clear intention to connect with the Records and seek guidance, knowledge, or understanding. It is crucial to approach this process with respect, humility, and pure intentions, seeking information that is aligned with your highest good and the highest good of all.

Meditation and alignment:

Engage in a deep meditative state to quiet the mind and connect with your higher self or spiritual guides. By stilling the mental chatter and grounding yourself in the present moment, you create a conducive environment to access higher realms of consciousness. Focus on your breath, relax your body, and visualize yourself surrounded by pure, loving energy.

Visualization and symbolism:

Use visualization techniques to imagine a gateway or entrance that leads to the Akashic Records. This can be a door, a book, a staircase, or any symbol that represents a pathway to the information you seek. Visualize this symbol and mentally affirm that it is opening up to reveal the vast knowledge and wisdom contained within the Records. Some people like to think of going up an elevator as if your consciousness is on a journey from the third dimension to the 5th-dimensional time-space, in which the records exist.

Once you arrive at your destination, give yourself totems like in the 2010 film "Inception." Each character had a unique personal object that helped them determine if they were in a dream or not. The totems had specific properties or behaviors that were known only to their owners. By observing the totem's behavior in a dream, they could confirm the dream state. For example, Dom Cobb (played by Leonardo DiCaprio) had a spinning top that would never stop spinning in a dream, but in reality, it would eventually topple over. You must find a sign specific to you that allows you to know whether or not you're in the records.

Ask questions and listen:

Once you feel connected and aligned with the Akashic Records, ask your questions silently or aloud, maintaining a focused and receptive state. Avoid yes/no questions. Instead, ask open-ended questions that encourage detailed and insightful responses. Example: "How do you think we could improve my relationship with such and such?" Be patient and allow the answers to come to you. It may manifest as thoughts, images, feelings, or intuitive insights. Trust your intuition and inner guidance as you receive the information.

Practice and patience:

Accessing the Akashic Records is a skill that can be developed and refined with practice. Regularly engage in meditation, visualization, and other metaphysical practices to strengthen your connection and expand your abilities. It is important to be patient with yourself and the process, as accessing the records may not always yield immediate or clear results. Trust that the information you seek will be revealed to you when the time is right.

Remember, accessing the Akashic Records requires respect, integrity, and a genuine desire for personal growth and spiritual evolution. It is a profound tool for self-discovery and accessing universal wisdom, but it should be approached with reverence and responsibility.

When trying to download knowledge from a higher source, it's important to open yourself up from limiting beliefs. Think back to when you were a child. You had an open mind and an unlimited imagination. Imagination flourishes the most when you are given that space to create and not be controlled but guided. Imagination is what allows you to have that highest potential. When you are controlled, you become limited. Children lose their vivid imagination that once seemed to connect them to a higher source.

Imagination is seen as a direct portal to the metaphysical realms, allowing individuals to tap into higher consciousness and access alternate dimensions of reality. Young children, unburdened by the conditioning and limitations imposed by society, possess a remarkable ability to traverse realms effortlessly. They converse with imaginary friends and manifest their desires effortlessly through their unfiltered Imagination. However, as children transition into the education system and societal structures, a systematic campaign begins to dampen their creative spark. Through standardized education, the system molds young minds to fit within predetermined frameworks, discouraging imagination and promoting conformity. Societal pressures and cultural expectations gradually erode the freedom of thought and expression that children once possessed. The pursuit of material wealth, social acceptance, and the fear of failure gradually consume their consciousness, leaving little room for the exploration of metaphysical realms.

As a result, the innate connection to the source becomes obscured, and the child's imagination, once vibrant and expansive, withers away. This connection can be rediscovered through inner work and self-exploration. Practices such as meditation, mindfulness, creative expression, and spiritual inquiry can help individuals reconnect with their inner child and access the wellspring of imagination that connects us back to the source. It's the power of imagination that allows us to access the Akasha.

CHAPTER EIGHT

COLLECTIVE CONSCIOUSNESS

WHAT IS CONSCIOUSNESS?

This is a question I ask myself, and honestly, I couldn't find a true answer. Consciousness is a complex and multifaceted phenomenon that has been explored and debated by philosophers and scientists for centuries. There's no universally accepted definition.

Most of us can agree that consciousness is a state of awareness or subjective experience of being aware of one's own thoughts, sensations, emotions, and the external world and having a sense of self and an understanding of one's surroundings.

We know that living organisms such as humans, animals and plants possess a form of consciousness, But can something inanimate, such as a rock, possess consciousness? Panpsychism proposes that consciousness is not solely a product of complex biological systems but a fundamental aspect of reality itself. Consciousness is not limited to humans or animals but extends to all entities, including inanimate objects like rocks.

Now, with that in mind, think in the context of how life on Earth started. Consciousness was present in some rudimentary form from the very beginning, even in the earliest form of matter. Rocks, being composed of atoms and molecules, would also possess some level of consciousness. Over billions of years, simple organic molecules combined to form self-replicating systems, which eventually led to the emergence of life in the form of single-celled organisms. This tells you that even primitive life forms possess a certain degree of consciousness.

The evolution of consciousness can be seen as a continuous process where simple conscious elements combine and interact, giving rise to more complex conscious entities. From this perspective, human consciousness is an emergent property of the intricate neural networks and information-processing systems in our brains. The prevailing scientific view is that consciousness emerges as a result of the complex interactions between brain activity, neural networks, and information processing.

There is substantial evidence to suggest that specific regions and networks in the brain play crucial roles in generating conscious experiences. Various studies have demonstrated correlations between specific brain activities and particular aspects of consciousness, such as perception, attention, and self-awareness. Additionally, alterations in brain function due to injury, disease, or the influence of substances can profoundly impact conscious experiences, further supporting the connection between the brain and consciousness.

Nevertheless, it's crucial to acknowledge that the exact mechanisms through which brain activity gives rise to consciousness remain uncertain. The "Hard problem of consciousness," as described by philosopher David Chalmers, refers to the challenge of understanding how and why subjective experiences arise from neural processes.

While consciousness appears to be intricately linked with the brain, some philosophers and theorists propose the existence of alternative or additional factors that may contribute to consciousness, such as quantum processes or non-material aspects of the mind. These ideas, however, are highly speculative and have yet to be empirically validated.

According to Gautama Buddha, consciousness is one of the five aggregates (skandhas) that make up our human experience. In Buddhist philosophy, consciousness is referred to as " Vijñāna" or "Vinnana." Buddha taught that consciousness is not an unchanging, permanent entity but rather a process that arises dependent on conditions. It is the awareness or knowing aspect of our experience.

Consciousness arises in dependence on sensory input and mental formations, such as thoughts, feelings, and perceptions. Buddha described consciousness as being interdependent and interconnected with other aspects of our existence, such as the body, feelings, perceptions, and mental formations. It is not separate or independent but arises due to various causes and conditions. Consciousness is said to arise and pass away in each moment, giving rise to the continuous flow of experience. Buddha emphasized the impermanent and insubstantial nature of consciousness. He taught that attachment to consciousness and identification with it leads to suffering because it perpetuates the illusion of a separate and enduring self.

Buddhist teachings encourage practitioners to cultivate mindfulness and insight meditation (Vipassana) to develop a direct understanding of the nature of consciousness and other aggregates. Through this practice, one can gain insight into the impermanence and non-self nature of consciousness, ultimately leading to liberation from suffering.

According to the Yogacara teachings, Alayavijnana, also known as the "Storehouse Consciousness," is a concept found in some Buddhist traditions, particularly in the Yogacara or Vijnanavada school. The term "Alaya" can be translated as "Storehouse" or "Repository," and "Vijnana" is often rendered as "Consciousness" or "Awareness." Alayavijnana is considered to be one of the eight consciousnesses in this school of thought.

Alayavijnana is a fundamental aspect of the mind that serves as a storehouse or repository for all the impressions, experiences, and karmic imprints accumulated throughout countless lifetimes.

It is seen as the basis for the arising of individual consciousness and is thought to underlie the other six consciousnesses, which include the five senses (sight, hearing, smell, taste, and touch) and the thinking mind.

The Alayavijnana is a relatively subtle and deep level of consciousness operating beneath the surface of our everyday awareness. This background of the mind is what Swiss psychiatrist Carl Jung considers to be "The unconsciousness."

THE COLLECTIVE UNCONSCIOUSNESS

The collective unconsciousness is a concept that Swiss psychiatrist Carl Jung developed. According to Jung, the collective unconsciousness refers to the deepest and most inaccessible part of the psyche that contains archetypes, which are universal symbolic representations or patterns of thought and behavior. Jung believed that the collective unconsciousness is inherited and shared by all human beings as a result of our common ancestral past. He suggested that it is distinct from the personal unconsciousness, which is unique to each individual and contains their personal experiences and memories.

The collective unconsciousness is said to manifest through various symbols and motifs found in myths, fairy tales, religious beliefs, and dreams. These symbols are believed to reflect universal human experiences and patterns of thought that have existed across cultures and throughout history. Jung's concept of the collective unconsciousness suggests that there are deeper layers of the human mind that transcend individual experiences and are connected to our shared humanity.

The concept of the collective unconsciousness, developed by Swiss psychiatrist Carl Jung and the Alayavijnana in Mahayana Buddhism share certain similarities. The collective unconsciousness and the

Alayavijnana propose the existence of a universal and interconnected consciousness that transcends individual experiences. They suggest that there is a deeper level of consciousness that underlies and connects all beings.

Both concepts suggest that this universal consciousness serves as a storehouse of information or a repository of collective experiences. It contains archetypal images, symbols, and patterns that influence individual experiences and behavior. This shared knowledge is not consciously accessible but can emerge in dreams, myths, and cultural expressions.

According to both Jungian psychology and Mahayana Buddhism, the collective unconsciousness and the Alayavijnana play a significant role in shaping individual experiences. They suggest that our thoughts, emotions, and behaviors are influenced by collective influences that we may not be fully aware of. These influences can manifest in the form of archetypal patterns, cultural conditioning, or karmic imprints.

Both concepts emphasize the transpersonal nature of consciousness. They go beyond the individual ego and recognize the existence of a larger, interconnected consciousness that transcends personal boundaries—implying that individuals are not isolated entities but part of a larger web of consciousness.

While both Alayavijnana and the collective unconsciousness explore deeper layers of consciousness and shared aspects of human experience, they differ in their origins, contents, and emphasis. The nature of consciousness in Alayavijnana is considered a foundational aspect of consciousness that serves as a storehouse for karmic imprints and experiences.

According to Carl Jung, the collective unconsciousness is a deeper layer of the psyche that contains shared archetypes, symbols, and universal patterns of human experience. Alayavijnana is believed to be a result of karmic accumulation across lifetimes and the basis for individual consciousness. Jung postulated that the collective unconsciousness is inherited and shared by all humans, stemming from the collective experiences of our ancestors. I believe in a way that the Buddhists have an understanding of what Jung describes as the collective unconsciousness.

In Mahayana Buddhism, a bodhisattva aspires to achieve enlightenment for the benefit of all sentient beings. They vow to postpone their own final liberation or enlightenment until all beings have been freed from suffering. This vow is known as the "Bodhisattva Vow" or the "Great Vow" and is a central concept in Mahayana Buddhism. The bodhisattva dedicates their efforts and spiritual practice to helping others on the path to liberation.

They strive to cultivate compassion, wisdom, and skillful means to alleviate suffering and guide all sentient beings toward enlightenment. The idea behind this vow is rooted in the belief that all beings are interconnected and that true liberation can only be attained when all beings are liberated. By postponing personal enlightenment, the Bodhisattva commits themselves to an altruistic path of service and compassion.

GENETIC MEMORY

The amount of information carried in one gram of DNA is quite remarkable. Deoxyribonucleic Acid is the genetic material found in living organisms. It contains the instructions necessary for the development, functioning, and reproduction of all known organisms. In terms of the storage capacity of DNA, it is estimated that one gram of DNA can store approximately 215 petabytes (215 million gigabytes) of data. This calculation is based on the fact that DNA is made up of four nucleotide bases: adenine (A), cytosine (C), guanine (G), and thymine (T). These bases can be arranged in different sequences, and each base can be represented by two bits of information (binary code: 00 for A, 01 for C, 10 for G, and 11 for T).

The amount of DNA in the human body can vary slightly from person to person, but on average, an adult human body contains approximately 50 to 100 trillion cells. Each cell, with the exception of mature red blood cells, contains a complete set of DNA. The total amount of DNA in each cell is typically around 6 billion base pairs.

Let's think outside the scientific box; our DNA could carry more than just biological information. It could potentially hold the imprints of our ancestors' experiences, memories, and even the collective consciousness of humanity.

DNA could be likened to a living library, storing not only our genetic makeup but a deeper tapestry of information for cosmic energy and universal wisdom, enabling us to tap into ancient knowledge or access ancestral memories through intuitive or spiritual practices.

One of my all-time favorite video game series is Assassins Creed, simply due to its intricate storyline. I won't get too deep into the back story of the game, but I will include genetic memory. Genetic memory is a central concept that drives the storyline and gameplay mechanics. The series introduces the idea that individuals can access the memories of their ancestors through their genetic code.

The game has fictional technology called the "Animus" that allows individuals known as "Assassins" to relive the memories of their ancestors. These memories are stored in the DNA of the present-day characters, and by connecting to the animus, they can explore and experience historical events from the perspectives of their ancestors.

The genetic memory concept suggests that the present-day characters can access the experiences and skills of these ancestors. This allows the modern Assassins to learn from the past, acquire abilities, and gain insights that aid them in their struggle against the Templars, a rival faction seeking control and domination. The animus acts as a virtual reality machine that reconstructs the memories of the ancestors by decoding and interpreting the genetic information stored within the user's DNA. By synchronizing with the animus, players control the main character and navigate through various historical settings and periods, such as the Third Crusade, Renaissance Italy, Colonial America, and more. This game makes me wonder if we can inherit memories from our ancestors.

The concept of inheriting memories from our ancestors is a topic of scientific and philosophical debate. From a scientific perspective, there is currently no empirical evidence to support the idea that we can directly inherit memories encoded in our DNA.

Memories are believed to be formed through complex neural connections in the brain. The specific details of an individual's experiences are not thought to be passed down through genetic material. However, there is an area of study known as epigenetics that explores how environmental factors and experiences can influence gene expression.

Epigenetic changes involve modifications to the structure of DNA or the proteins associated with it, which can affect how genes are activated or suppressed. Some researchers propose that these epigenetic modifications could potentially transmit information across generations, allowing certain traits or predispositions to be inherited.

Epigenetic programming has been shown to play a role in the memory consolidation of fear, pleasure, depression, and anxiety associated with particular stimuli. One could speculate that this could be the mechanism by which ancestral environments are passed down to offspring.

One example of an experiment that demonstrated the inheritance of fear of certain smells across generations in mice is the study conducted by Dias and Ressler in 2013. This experiment involved conditioning mice to associate a specific odor, acetophenone, with a foot shock. The researchers conditioned a group of male mice to associate the smell of acetophenone with a foot shock. The mice were exposed to the odor of acetophenone and simultaneously received a mild electric foot shock. This process was repeated several times to establish a fear response to the smell.

After conditioning, the researchers assessed the fear response of the conditioned mice. They exposed the mice to the smell of acetophenone and observed their behavioral and physiological responses, such as freezing behavior (indicative of fear) and stress hormone release. The male mice were then bred with female mice who had never been exposed to the conditioning or the acetophenone smell. The resulting offspring, referred to as the F1 generation, had no direct exposure to the odor or foot shock.

The F1 generation mice were exposed to the acetophenone smell, and their fear response was evaluated. Despite not having undergone conditioning themselves, they displayed a fear response similar to that of their fathers. This suggested the inheritance of the fear response across generations. To investigate the underlying mechanisms, the researchers examined epigenetic modifications in the sperm cells of the conditioned male mice. Specifically, they looked for changes in DNA methylation, a common epigenetic modification that can affect gene expression.

Researchers found alterations in DNA methylation patterns in certain genes associated with the odorant receptor system in the olfactory system of the conditioned male mice. These changes were indicative of epigenetic modifications resulting from the conditioning experience.

Remarkably, the altered DNA methylation patterns were also observed in the sperm cells of the F1 generation mice. This suggested that the offspring inherited the epigenetic changes induced by the conditioning experience. The F1 generation mice were bred to produce a second generation of offspring, known as the F2 generation. Like the F1 mice, the F2 generation exhibited a heightened fear response to the acetophenone smell despite never having been conditioned or directly exposed to the odor or foot shock.

Overall, this experiment demonstrated that the fear response to a specific smell (acetophenone) could be inherited across multiple generations in mice. It provided insights into the complex interplay between environmental experiences, such as conditioning, and epigenetic modifications, specifically DNA methylation, which may contribute to the transgenerational transmission of fear-related behaviors.

Another study that provided valuable insights into the field of epigenetics was The Dutch Hunger Winter Study, also known as the Dutch Famine Study. This landmark research project investigated the long-term health effects of prenatal exposure to severe famine during World War II and how environmental factors can influence gene expression and health outcomes later in life.

During the winter of 1944-1945, the Nazi occupation of the Netherlands led to a blockade that severely restricted food supplies to the western regions of the country. As a result, the population experienced a period of extreme famine known as the Dutch Hunger Winter. Pregnant women during this time were exposed to severe nutritional deprivation, which had a profound impact on their health and the development of their unborn children.

The Dutch Hunger Winter Study utilized data collected from individuals who were in utero during the famine period. Researchers tracked the health outcomes of these individuals throughout their lives and compared them to individuals born before or after the famine.

The study revealed several significant findings. Prenatal exposure to famine was associated with a higher risk of chronic diseases, including obesity, diabetes, cardiovascular disease, and certain types of cancer. These findings indicated that the effects of prenatal malnutrition could persist into adulthood.

The study found evidence of epigenetic changes in individuals exposed to famine. The researchers observed alterations in DNA methylation patterns, which play a crucial role in gene regulation. The study also revealed the transgenerational effects of the famine. The children of individuals who experienced prenatal famine were found to have a higher prevalence of certain health conditions, suggesting that the effects of malnutrition could be passed down to subsequent generations.

The Dutch Hunger Winter Study highlighted the importance of the prenatal environment in shaping long-term health outcomes. It demonstrated that early-life nutritional experiences can have a lasting impact on an individual's health and the health of future generations. The epigenetic changes observed in this study provided valuable insights into the mechanisms by which environmental factors can influence gene expression and contribute to disease susceptibility.

Overall, the Dutch Hunger Winter Study serves as a significant contribution to the field of epigenetics, deepening our understanding of the complex interplay between genetics and environmental factors in shaping human health.

One could hypothesize that the experiences and epigenetic modifications of past generations, such as those observed in the Dutch Hunger Winter Study, as well as the transmission of fear in the mouse experiment, become imprinted in the collective consciousness. This collective pool of knowledge or energy could potentially influence the experiences and behaviors of subsequent generations.

THE COLLECTIVE

The concept of collective consciousness was coined by French sociologist Emile Durkheim. Durkheim proposed that collective consciousness refers to the shared beliefs, values, norms, and knowledge that exist within a society or social group. It represents the collective identity and shared understanding of a community or culture. The collective consciousness encompasses the ideas, attitudes, and perspectives that members of a society commonly hold, and it shapes their social interactions and behaviors. Durkheim argued that collective consciousness emerges from social integration and shared experiences within a group. It influences individuals' thoughts, emotions, and actions, creating a sense of cohesion and solidarity. The collective consciousness is often associated with social norms and moral values that guide individual behavior, as well as the collective sense of identity and belonging. Metaphysically, collective consciousness refers to the idea that a higher level of awareness emerges when individuals come together, forming a collective entity. It implies that the collective entity has a distinct consciousness that transcends the individual minds of its members. This shared consciousness can potentially influence the thoughts, emotions, and behaviors of individuals within the group, creating a sense of unity and shared identity. Human beings are interconnected on a profound level.

Individual thoughts, emotions, and energies are not confined within the boundaries of our physical bodies but are part of a broader, shared consciousness. This interconnectedness is said to transcend time and space, allowing for the exchange and transmission of information on a non-local level.

It was once widely believed that running a mile in less than four minutes was physically impossible for humans. However, on May 6, 1954, Roger Bannister, a British middle-distance runner, achieved this feat, running a mile in 3 minutes and 59.4 seconds. Bannister's accomplishment shattered the perceived barrier, and it was considered a significant milestone in the history of sports. What's interesting about this event is the impact it had on the collective consciousness.

When Bannister broke the 4-minute mile barrier, it challenged the collective consciousness of the time, proving that what was once believed to be impossible was indeed achievable. This breakthrough had a profound psychological effect on athletes and the public at large.

Bannister's achievement sparked a wave of belief and motivation among other runners. In the years following his record-breaking run, several athletes around the world started breaking the 4-minute mile barrier. Once the collective consciousness shifted to accept the possibility, more people were able to tap into their potential and accomplish what was previously considered unattainable. It demonstrated the power of shared belief systems and how they can influence human performance and achievement.

This example illustrates how collective consciousness can shape individual and collective behavior. When a widely held belief is challenged or shattered, it opens up new possibilities and expands the limits of what people believe is possible. It highlights the interplay between individual achievements and the broader social context in which it takes place.

The Hundredth Monkey Experiment is a thought-provoking concept that originated from an anecdotal account in the 1950s. The experiment was said to involve a group of snow monkeys on a Japanese island who learned to wash sweet potatoes to remove the dirt before eating them.

According to the story, between 1952 and 1953, primatologists conducted a behavioral study that gave a troop of Japanese Macaque (*Macaca fuscata*), also known as the snow monkey with sweet potatoes. The monkeys enjoyed the taste of sweet potatoes but didn't like the taste of sand. One of the young female monkeys figured out that she could wash the sweet potatoes in the water to improve the taste of the sweet potatoes. She taught this trick to her mother and playmates, who shared the method with their companions. The scientists observed that the younger monkey would automatically wash their sweet potatoes, but some of the older ones were still hesitant about this new method. In the autumn of 1958, scientists noticed a larger number of snow monkeys washing their sweet potatoes. The exact number was unknown; the hypothetical number was 99, and then out of nowhere, the 100th monkey started to wash their sweet potato. This added energy created a breakthrough for the collective; every monkey within the troop washed their sweet potatoes before eating. This behavior spontaneously spread to other monkeys on neighboring islands, who never had any contact with the original colony that discovered the method. This phenomenon suggests that when a limited number of individuals learn a new method, the old method remains the conscious property of the individuals. However, when more contribute to the new idea, the collective field is strengthened, allowing those who are willing to accept the new idea.

From this perspective, the Hundredth Monkey Experiment serves as a metaphorical reminder of the power of our individual and collective choices. It suggests that as we evolve and expand our consciousness, we contribute to the overall growth and transformation of humanity. It encourages us to be mindful of the thoughts and beliefs we hold, as they can have a ripple effect on the collective consciousness. This concept aligns with various beliefs, such as the law of attraction, morphic resonance, or the concept of the collective unconscious proposed by Carl Jung.

However, it's important to note that the Hundredth Monkey Experiment has been criticized for its lack of scientific rigor and empirical evidence. Some argue that the anecdotal story may have been embellished or misunderstood over time. While the concept is intriguing, it should be approached with a degree of skepticism and critical thinking.

During the start of the COVID-19 pandemic, I posted a very controversial video about how I believed if we shifted our thoughts, the disease would go away to a certain extent. I received a lot of backlash from people saying, "You can't manifest a virus away; that's not how viruses work." The collective didn't understand where I was coming from, but the few who did know exactly where I was going with that thought process. I looked at the virus as a childhood boogieman; the more energy you give it, the longer it lingers. Once you stop believing in it, it disappears. During the start of the pandemic, the media controlled the collective, constantly fear-mongering every time we turned on the TV, keeping the boogeyman relevant.

I stopped watching the media and decided to take up hiking, traveling across the Appalachian region of the United States. States like Georgia didn't have any COVID restrictions. It felt illegal to walk around. Eerie as it was, it was nice to feel a bit of normalcy. I knew the world would eventually get back to normal once we collectively diverted our attention away from the media.

I believed that we could effectively shift the energetic dynamics surrounding COVID-19 when we stopped fixating on the negative aspects of the pandemic, such as fear, anxiety, and despair, which unintentionally perpetuate its presence.

When we collectively shift our attention toward positive aspects of life and direct our energy towards The energy we emit through our thoughts, beliefs, and emotions attract similar experiences into our reality. By withdrawing attention from the disease and focusing on health, vitality, and overall well-being, we alter the vibrational frequency at which we collectively operate. In doing so, we create a reality in which the virus struggles to sustain itself, ultimately diminishing its impact.

If you look at the world today, COVID-19 still exists as it always will, but it isn't a dominating factor in our lives. We don't have to stand six feet apart; masks are only worn by choice, and the media hardly ever talks about it anymore.

Now, one can argue we reached herd immunity due to the vaccine, and one can also play devil's advocate by stating the fact that the virus continued to mutate. People who were vaccinated still were impacted by the virus. My thoughts personally remain the same. I believe humanity collectively shifted its consciousness away from the virus.

How to Benefit from the Collective

Humanity exists within a multidimensional matrix of interconnected energies, where our individual, collective thoughts and beliefs contribute to the creation of our shared reality. The first step towards shifting the collective consciousness lies in recognizing the existence of this matrix and understanding the extent to which our thoughts and beliefs shape our experiences. We have to change what we are uploading and downloading from the collective field.

Breaking free from the limiting beliefs imposed by society's status quo is a crucial aspect of this transformative process. These beliefs are often designed to maintain control and suppress the innate potential of individuals. They confine us to a narrow perception of reality, preventing us from exploring the depths of our consciousness and realizing our true capabilities.

To initiate a shift in collective consciousness, individuals must embark on an inner journey of self- discovery and personal liberation. This involves breaking free of the cognitive dissonance, questioning societal narratives, challenging the accepted truths, and developing alternative perspectives.

By questioning the status quo, we begin to unravel the layers of conditioning that have influenced our thoughts and beliefs, paving the way for new possibilities.

As individuals awaken to their true nature and expand their consciousness, a ripple effect occurs. Like-minded individuals gravitate towards one another, forming communities and networks that share similar visions of a better reality. These groups become catalysts for change, fostering the emergence of a collective consciousness that transcends the limitations of the prevailing paradigm.

In this new paradigm, cooperation, empathy, and unity become the guiding principles. As the collective consciousness shifts, so does the shared reality. The manifestation of a better world becomes possible as the focus shifts from competition and division to collaboration and interconnectedness.

The power of intention and visualization plays a vital role in this process. By collectively envisioning a harmonious and abundant future, humanity strengthens the energetic currents that shape our reality. Visualization practices, meditation, and other metaphysical techniques become tools for aligning individual and collective consciousness, amplifying the desired outcomes. Additionally, exploring esoteric knowledge and ancient wisdom can aid in this transformative journey. Hidden truths about the nature of reality, consciousness, and the interplay of energies can empower individuals to navigate the multidimensional matrix with clarity and purpose. As this knowledge spreads and gains wider acceptance, it acts as a catalyst for further shifts in collective consciousness.

It is essential to acknowledge that this process may encounter resistance from established power structures that seek to maintain control. However, by staying committed to the pursuit of truth, liberation, and positive transformation, humanity can overcome these obstacles. The collective consciousness becomes a force, fostering systemic change and paving the way for a new era of enlightenment.

CHAPTER NINE

TRUST YOUR INTUITION

WHAT IS INTUITION?

Intuition refers to a form of knowledge or understanding that is obtained without conscious reasoning or logical analysis. It is often described as a gut feeling, a hunch, or an instinctive understanding of something, even when there may not be concrete evidence or logical reasoning to support it.

Intuition can manifest in various ways, such as a sudden insight, a feeling of certainty, or a sense of knowing. It can be applied to different areas of life, including decision-making, problem-solving, creativity, and interpersonal interactions. People may rely on intuition to make quick judgments, navigate uncertain situations, or tap into their creativity.

Intuition allows individuals to tap into a realm of higher wisdom, spiritual guidance, or the collective unconscious. It is believed to be a way of accessing profound truths, hidden knowledge, or insights about the nature of reality, existence, and the self. In trusting our instincts, we develop a relationship with our higher self—a partnership in which we consciously align ourselves with the innate wisdom that flows through us. By embracing this connection, we can cultivate a deep sense of trust and confidence in the decisions we make, knowing that they arise from a profound source of knowledge and insight. Our higher self is an expansive, transcendent aspect of our being that exists beyond the confines of time and space. It encompasses our innate wisdom, accumulated knowledge, and intuitive insights. It is through this higher self that we tap into a broader consciousness, allowing us to perceive and understand things that may lie beyond our conscious awareness.

When we encounter a situation that requires a decision, our higher self may have already traversed the realm of possibilities and potential outcomes, making a choice based on its vast understanding of our unique path and purpose. This choice is then communicated to our conscious awareness through the conduit of our gut feeling or instinct, which we should never ignore. Trusting our gut feelings is an act of surrendering to the wisdom of our higher self.

It means acknowledging that there is a depth of knowledge and understanding within us that surpasses our conscious mind's limitations. By allowing ourselves to listen and be receptive to this inner guidance, we tap into a wellspring of wisdom that can inform our decisions and ultimately lead us toward paths aligned with our highest good.

Characteristics of Intuition

Intuition operates beyond the realm of conscious reasoning and logic. It is a non-analytical mode of knowing that bypasses conscious thought processes. Intuitive insights can arise quickly and spontaneously, often appearing as sudden flashes or hunches.

They can occur without deliberate effort or extended contemplation. Sometimes, you will see people make a spontaneous life-changing decision that makes no sense from an outside perspective. It might even make no sense to the person making the decision.

Someone's intuition may have them quit their job and leave their comfort zone without really knowing why, but they feel an internal calling that's moving them toward something else, even if they have no real plan. The plan usually involves going with the flow and trusting whatever the universe has in store for you.

Someone who instantly comes to my mind is Jack Dawson. The fictional character from the movie Titanic, portrayed by Leonardo DiCaprio, is depicted as someone who goes with the flow of the universe and follows his intuition. Jack is quoted as saying, "I figure life's a gift, and I don't intend on wasting it. You never know what hand you're gonna get dealt next. You learn to take life as it comes at you to make each day count." This quote echoes the concept of carpe diem, which means "Seize the day." Jack's philosophy aligns with this idea of living in the present, making the most of every moment, and not allowing life's uncertainties to hinder his pursuit of happiness. Jack's journey from being homeless to mingling with first-class passengers and sipping champagne can be seen as a testament to his trusting nature and his ability to seize opportunities. From the moment Jack boards the Titanic, he exhibits a carefree and adventurous spirit. He doesn't adhere to the strict social divisions of the ship and instead embraces the freedom to explore and interact with people from all walks of life.

This openness allows him to meet Rose DeWitt Bukater, the first-class passenger, and their subsequent connection becomes a pivotal turning point in his life. Jack's character embodies a sense of spontaneity and living in the present moment. Rather than being burdened by his circumstances, he takes each day as it comes and trusts his instincts to guide him.

Now I get it: Jack is a fictional character. However, suppose you've ever encountered anyone who truly followed their intuition. In that case, they will most likely tell you they've lived a life that they never could've imagined they would ever live because they're usually the ones who broke free of the social norms and trusted whatever the universe has in store for them. Intuition often manifests as non-verbal cues or feelings rather than explicit thoughts or logical statements. It may involve sensations, emotions or bodily reactions that guide decision-making.

One in particular is a gut feeling; sometimes, we can meet someone for the first time, but we get this feeling in our gut that something is off about them. We might not realize this, but our bodies have the capability of picking up energy before we even enter a room.

1. The Crown Chakra

2. The Third Eye Chakra

3. The Throat Chakra

4. The Heart Chakra

5. The Solar Plexus Chakra

6. The Sacral Chakra

7. The Base/Root Chakra

The stomach knows before your brain, and your stomach is home to your solar plexus chakra, the seat of the soul. It guides you through this physical realm with intuition and the gut feelings you receive. The gut-brain axis is a bidirectional communication pathway between the gut and the brain, facilitated by a network of nerves, hormones, and chemical messengers. The stomach, being a crucial part of the gut, communicates with the brain through this axis, allowing for the exchange of information and signals.

Research has shown that humans and other animals carry a diverse community of micro-organisms on their skin, in their mouths, and within their gastrointestinal and respiratory tracts. These micro-organisms, collectively known as the human microbiota, play important roles in various aspects of human health, including digestion, immune function, and protection against pathogens and hidden danger.

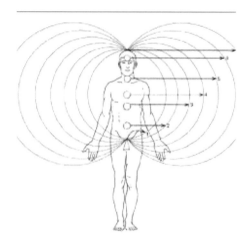

The microbial aura or cloud refers to the dispersal of these microorganisms into the surrounding environment. Studies have demonstrated that individuals emit a unique blend of micro-organisms. This cloud of microbes can be detected and analyzed in the immediate vicinity of a person.

Each micro-organism emits its unique energetic signature, and when combined, it creates a collective energy field within a given space. This microbial aura is believed to hold valuable information and vibrations that can be sensed or read by individuals who are attuned to subtle energies.

Your body is tapping into and interpreting the energetic imprints left behind by the microbial cloud and other energetic influences present within that space. One may perceive the vibrations of a room through intuition or extrasensory perception. They might pick up on the overall "Feel" or atmosphere of the space, influenced by the collective microbial energy, emotional residues, and other subtle energies present. Your body might sense whether the space feels vibrant, stagnant, harmonious, or imbalanced based on the interactions and dynamics of the microbial cloud.

Variations in the energy field might be indicative of the health, vitality, and overall balance of the micro-organisms present. When the body feels an imbalance, it will send subtle cues that might manifest as a feeling of warmth, tingling, heaviness, lightness, or other sensations. The human body is said to emit an electromagnetic field, which interacts with the energetic fields of others and the environment. The microbiome, as a vital component of our physical body, contributes to this overall energy field. According to the research conducted by the HeartMath Institute, the heart also appears to play a significant role in the process of making intuitive decisions.

Traditionally, intuition has been associated with the mind or the brain. However, the HeartMath Institute suggests that the heart also possesses its own intelligence and can influence our decision-making process. This concept is known as "Heart Intelligence" or "Heart Intuition."

The Institute's research suggests that the heart communicates with the brain and other parts of the body through electromagnetic signals. These signals can have an impact on our perceptions, emotions, and decision-making abilities. In fact, the heart's electromagnetic field is believed to be the most powerful electromagnetic field produced by the human body, and it can extend several feet beyond the body.

When it comes to intuitive decision-making, the HeartMath Institute's research indicates that the heart tends to react differently compared to analytical thinking. While analytical thinking involves a logical and linear process, intuition often arises as a sudden insight or a gut feeling.

According to the HeartMath Institute, when individuals make intuitive decisions, the heart's signals can influence the brain's processing and perception. It is believed that the heart's signals can reach the brain before the brain processes information from the external environment, allowing the heart's intuitive input to guide the decision-making process. In addition to its role in intuition, the HeartMath Institute's research also suggests that the heart can influence our emotions and overall well-being. They have developed techniques and technologies, such as Heart Rate Variability (HRV) training, to help individuals regulate their heart rhythms and enhance their heart coherence. Heart coherence refers to a state where the heart, brain, and other physiological systems are in a synchronized and balanced state, leading to improved cognitive function, emotional stability, and intuition.

Ultimately, whether you rely on your heart or your intuition, it's essential to balance it with rational thinking and logical analysis. Integrating both heart-based intuition and analytical reasoning can provide a more comprehensive approach to decision-making and problem-solving. One can easily be convinced that they're following their intuition when they're following their ego.

Is It Intuition or Ego?

I personally like to think of ego as Loki in Norse mythology and intuition as his brother Thor. In the context of psychological archetypes, Loki and Thor can be seen as representations of different aspects of the human psyche. Loki is often associated with the ego, while Thor can be linked to intuition. The ego, in psychological terms, represents the conscious mind, the sense of self, and the part of us that interacts with the external world. Loki, the god of mischief in Norse mythology, embodies various traits associated with the ego. He is cunning and manipulative and often acts out of self-interest, seeking personal gain or validation. Loki is known for his shape-shifting abilities, which symbolize the adaptability and versatility of the ego.

Intuition, on the other hand, is associated with the unconscious mind and represents a deeper knowing beyond rational thought. Thor, the god of thunder, is often depicted as a warrior who relies on his instincts, strength, and intuitive understanding of situations. He is direct, straightforward, and acts with a strong sense of purpose. Thor's actions are not driven by personal gain but by a desire to protect and uphold order.

Loki's ultimate downfall can be attributed to his tendency to follow his ego. By constantly seeking to manipulate situations for his benefit, he often creates chaos and brings about negative consequences for himself and others. His actions are often short-sighted and driven by a desire for personal power and recognition. In contrast, Thor, who embodies intuition, acts with a clearer sense of purpose and aligns his actions with a greater understanding of the world and its order.

Thor, as intuition, highlights the importance of self-awareness and the impact of one's motivations on one's actions. Thor's intuitive and purpose-driven actions lead to a more positive and fulfilling path in the long run. While Loki's ego-driven behavior might lead to temporary gains, it ultimately results in his defeat and downfall.

The theme of ego versus intuition is a common motif in various mythologies and stories. Characters driven by ego often face internal struggles and external challenges that lead to their downfall, while those guided by intuition tend to make more informed and positive decisions that benefit themselves and the greater good.

The ego is notorious for tricking one into believing it is intuition because the ego doesn't like change. It is designed to keep you safe in your comfort zone. Distinguishing between intuition and ego can sometimes be challenging, as they can both influence our thoughts and decisions, but how can one tell the difference?

Let's start with the source: intuition often arises from a deeper, subconscious part of ourselves, drawing on our past experiences, knowledge, and wisdom. It can provide insights that go beyond our conscious awareness. On the other hand, ego is associated with our sense of self, identity, and desires. It tends to be driven by personal preferences, fears, and the need for validation.

Intuition tends to guide us towards choices that align with our authentic selves and higher good. It may focus on overall well-being, growth, and harmony. Conversely, the ego is more concerned with self-preservation, status, and satisfying immediate desires. It can be driven by fears, insecurities, and the need to prove oneself. Intuition often feels calm, confident, peaceful, and centered. It may provide a sense of clarity and inner knowing. It doesn't try to justify or prove its own truth; it will often leave you with a simple message or sentence.

Ego, on the other hand, can be associated with stronger emotions such as pride, defensiveness, competitiveness, or a sense of superiority. Intuition is often aligned with our authentic selves and values, representing our truest desires and aspirations. It can guide us towards choices that resonate deeply with who we are. Ego, on the other hand, can be influenced by societal expectations, external validation, and the need to conform or impress others.

Intuition often considers the long-term consequences and benefits, even if it requires sacrifices or patience in the present. Ego tends to prioritize immediate gratification or short-term gains without necessarily considering the broader impact.

Intuition often arises in moments of stillness, when the mind is calm and free from excessive mental chatter. Ego, on the other hand, can be associated with a louder inner dialogue, self-talk, and the need for constant validation or recognition. If your thoughts continue to change about a certain decision, it is most likely your ego.

How to Use Your Intuition

Intuition can indeed be compared to a muscle in the sense that it can be strengthened through use and can weaken or atrophy when neglected. If you neglect or ignore your intuition for prolonged periods, it may start to weaken or diminish. This is similar to how a muscle that is not exercised regularly can lose strength and undergo atrophy. When you consistently rely on logic or ignore your gut instincts, you may find it harder to access your intuitive abilities when you need them. The signals or insights that were once readily available may become faint or difficult to discern. My career in the fire department has truly transformed my intuition. Before joining the department, I was a sheltered kid raised in the suburbs of Bowie, Maryland. Back then, I lacked 'street smarts' and awareness of potentially dangerous situations that could jeopardize my life.

However, being a firefighter and an Emergency Medical Technician (EMT) has taught me the vital role of intuition in making split-second decisions that profoundly impact both our lives and the public we serve. This intuitive sense is honed through a combination of training, experience, and exposure to diverse emergency scenarios.

Over the years, I've come to rely on my gut feeling, which has been instrumental in saving lives, averting danger, and even excelling in tests. Simply trusting my instinct and going with my initial choice has proven to be effective time and time again.

Your inner guidance is an extension of the universe and will never steer you wrong. Recognizing and understanding your intuition can be a valuable skill in decision-making and navigating various aspects of life. Start by developing self-awareness and paying attention to your thoughts, feelings, and bodily sensations. Trusting and acting upon these intuitive prompts can reinforce your intuitive abilities. Practice discerning between fear-based thoughts and genuine intuitive guidance. Fear-based thoughts often stem from past experiences, conditioning, or worries about the future. They tend to be repetitive, anxious, negative, and rooted in self-doubt or limiting beliefs. By understanding the nature of fear-based thoughts, you can start identifying their patterns and tendencies.

Fear-based thoughts often trigger physical sensations like tension, tightness, or discomfort in your body. Intuitive guidance, however, tends to be accompanied by a sense of ease, relaxation, or a gentle expansion within. Pay attention to how your body reacts when different thoughts or ideas arise.

Look back on past situations where you followed fear-based thoughts versus intuitive guidance. Examine the outcomes and how you felt during those experiences. This reflection can provide valuable insights into the differences between fear-based thoughts and genuine intuitive guidance. Engage in exercises that stimulate and develop your intuitive senses. For example, practice guessing who is calling before answering the phone or try to sense the contents of a closed box without opening it. At work, I have a favorite exercise that involves guessing a patient's blood pressure before actually measuring it, and I've found that I'm often quite accurate. This exercise not only strengthens my intuition but also enables me to make swift decisions when treating future patients who exhibit similar symptoms.

Additionally, in moments of uncertainty or when I find myself at a crossroads, I turn to drawing tarot cards. Randomly shuffling the cards and observing which ones fall out has become a way for me to tap into my intuition and gain insight into the direction I should take next. It's like my intuition guiding me towards the right path.

When it comes to intuition, you must actively listen to your inner voice and the subtle messages it conveys. This requires slowing down, being present, and giving yourself the space to receive and interpret intuitive insights. Regular meditation can help quiet your mind, enhance your awareness, and open channels for intuitive insights to flow.

Mindfulness practices cultivate present-moment awareness, allowing you to tune in to subtle signals and sensations. These practices help you observe your thoughts, emotions, and physical sensations without judgment. With increased self-awareness, you can start recognizing when fear-based thoughts arise and how they differ from intuitive guidance.

Regularly journaling your thoughts, feelings, and experiences can help you become more aware of your intuitive nudges. Reviewing your entries can reveal patterns and connections that may deepen your intuitive understanding. One should also listen to their dreams. Dreams are intricately connected to our intuition; dreams unravel the hidden meanings deep within ourselves.

In the realm of dreams, our subconscious mind weaves intricate tapestries, blending symbols, emotions, and experiences into a vivid and often enigmatic landscape. It is within this ethereal realm that our intuition speaks to us, guiding us toward self-discovery, growth, and enlightenment. Dreams have the ability to bypass the limitations of our conscious mind, delving into the recesses of our psyche where our deepest thoughts, desires, fears, and unresolved issues reside. They serve as a direct line of communication with our intuition, offering glimpses into the profound wisdom that lies within us.

While awake, the noise of everyday life and the distractions of the external world often drown out the subtle whispers of our intuition. However, when we enter the realm of dreams, we are receptive to the messages that our intuition conveys.

Dreams manifest as symbols and archetypes that speak a language unique to our individual subconscious. They possess a profound capacity to tap into our collective unconscious, drawing upon universal imagery and mythic motifs.

This symbolic language often defies conventional logic and linear interpretation, instead engaging the intuitive and imaginative aspects of our consciousness. Through dreams, our intuition communicates in the language of symbols, urging us to explore deeper levels of self-awareness and to confront the shadow aspects of our being. When we engage with our dreams and actively seek to understand their hidden meanings, we embark on a journey of self-discovery.

Each dream holds within it a treasure trove of insights and revelations waiting to be unearthed. Through dream analysis and introspection, we can decipher the metaphoric messages presented to us, deciphering the cryptic codes that our intuition employs. Dreams act as a mirror, reflecting our innermost thoughts, emotions, and subconscious patterns. They reveal aspects of ourselves that may have eluded our conscious awareness, bringing to light unresolved conflicts, unexpressed desires, or hidden potentials. Dreams have the capacity to illuminate our blind spots and challenge our preconceived notions, encouraging us to explore alternative perspectives and expand our understanding of self. In order to fully embrace the connection between dreams and intuition, one must approach them with a sense of curiosity, openness, and trust. By cultivating a receptive mindset and maintaining a dream journal to record and reflect upon our dreams, we create a bridge to our intuition, strengthening the link between the conscious and subconscious realms. This practice enhances our ability to recognize patterns, symbols, and recurring themes within our dreams, enabling us to extract valuable insights and apply them to our waking lives.

CHAPTER TEN

REDIRECTION

MY REDIRECTION STORY

During the time when I was striving for a promotion within the fire department, I had a significant experience with redirection. The fire department promotional exams were quite demanding, requiring a comprehensive list of credentials and a flawless knowledge of Standard Operating Procedures (SOPs) and tactical operations.

Studying for these exams felt almost like preparing for law school due to the sheer volume of material I needed to retain. The first test I focused on was the Fire Specialist exam, which was not as intense as the lieutenant's exam, but there was some overlap in the study material, allowing me to prepare for both simultaneously. I began my preparations in February, with the Fire Specialist test scheduled for October and the lieutenant's exam in December.

To master the material, I used various study techniques. I created over a thousand flashcards and even converted the SOPs into audio format, which I listened to daily during my commutes to and from work. As the test dates drew nearer, I grew more confident with the amount of effort and time I had invested in studying. Finally, the day of the Fire Specialist exam arrived, and although I experienced some test anxiety initially, it quickly dissipated as I began to see the answers right in front of me during the test. The hours spent listening to the SOPs appeared to have paid off. After completing the test, I felt quite confident that I had passed. As people finished early, they started discussing their answers, and someone mentioned "Freebee answers" at the back of the test. I instantly realized that I hadn't seen any such answers.

A few days before the scores were released, my buddy from the academy called me and informed me about the free answers that were on the back of the test, which I had missed. When the scores finally came out, my heart sank -I had received a disappointing 68%, falling short of making the list.

It was frustrating to know that all I needed was a 72% to succeed, and I missed it simply because I hadn't paid attention and flipped through the booklet properly. I couldn't help but think about how much higher I could have scored if I had seen those additional answers. However, as they say, "Should've, could've, would've, but you didn't." Feeling defeated and lacking the confidence and motivation to continue studying for the lieutenant position, I pushed myself to persevere nonetheless. However, midway through my preparation for the test, a profound realization struck me like an epiphany. I came to the realization that my time in this pursuit had run its course, and I no longer wanted to pursue the path of becoming a lieutenant.

This moment of clarity led me to reflect deeply on my life's purpose and my journey within the fire department. It became evident to me that being a firefighter was never a true passion of mine. The decision to become a firefighter was primarily driven by the responsibility of having my son at the young age of 21 and feeling the need to provide for him and my family. During this reflective period, my neighbor, Mr. Ronnie, played a pivotal role in guiding me through the process.

Being a deputy chief with the DC fire department, he had valuable connections with neighboring jurisdictions, one of them being Prince George's County, the place where I was born and raised. Mr. Ronnie suggested that Prince George's County was hiring, and he encouraged me to start preparing for the Candidate Physical Ability Test (CPAT). He assured me that once I passed the test, he would assist me in the rest of the process. The first hurdle was the written exam, which I managed to pass without any problems. With my determination, I embarked on rigorous training sessions for the CPAT, working alongside my dad and attending training sessions held on Wednesday afternoons and Saturday mornings. After undergoing six weeks of training, I felt confident enough to attempt the CPAT (Candidate Physical Ability Test) on its first practice run. Passing this practice run would grant me a certificate valid for a year, allowing me to apply to other jurisdictions without having to retake the test. My initial try at the CPAT resulted in a time-out, but on the second attempt, I successfully passed with 30 seconds to spare. It felt like conquering Mount Everest, and I believed that with Mr. Ronnie's support, the path ahead would be smooth sailing.

Mr. Ronnie stayed true to his promise and introduced me to his friend Jonathan Bolden (JB), the chief of PGFD volunteer station 38 Chapel Oaks. JB welcomed me into his station, enabling me to obtain my Emergency Medical Technician (EMT) certification. Understanding that many people struggle with the EMT, JB wanted me to complete it before the fire academy to alleviate the stress during the fire training.

With the EMT course running from August to December, my son's due date was set for September. However, things didn't go as planned when I failed my first EMT test. The Maryland Fire Rescue Institute only allows three retakes, and with the clock ticking, I failed the second test as well, which meant another failure would lead to dismissal from the program.

Feeling disheartened, I turned to the universe for a sign. As I made this plea, the TV show "HOUSE M.D" played in the background, and when I heard sirens on the show, I looked up and saw an ambulance driving on the screen. It was a moment of clarity, a message from the universe as if assuring me that I was on the right path. From that point on, I never failed another test, successfully obtaining my EMT certification.

Despite these accomplishments, my journey took an unexpected turn when I learned that I wasn't selected for the PG County Fire Academy due to discrepancies in my background booklet. Attempting to rectify the issue, I reached out to my background investigator, but he was on vacation, leaving me unable to resolve the matter in time to attend the academy. My mother tried to console me, suggesting that perhaps it wasn't meant to be with that department and that the universe might have protected me from potential harm. However, I was focused on being hired and applied to multiple jurisdictions with no success until I received the call from the Baltimore County Fire Department.

Before starting the academy with Baltimore County, I saw news about a firefighter in PG County who was killed while checking on a welfare call. This tragic event brought my mother's words back to my mind, and I considered that the universe might have redirected me from that path to safeguard me from such a fate. This tragedy brought to mind an anecdote from the Zhuangzi, an ancient Chinese philosophical text. The story of the lost horse is used to convey the idea that events that initially appear unfortunate may, in fact, be blessings in disguise, and the reverse can also be true.

Here's the essence of the story:

> "Once upon a time, there was a farmer in ancient China who owned a beautiful horse. One day, this horse managed to escape from the farmer's stable and ran away to the neighboring kingdom. Upon hearing this, the farmer's neighbors came to console him, saying, "What a misfortune! You have lost your most valuable possession, your horse."

The farmer, however, responded with calmness, saying, "Maybe it's a blessing, maybe it's a curse. Who knows?" After some time, the lost horse returned to the farmer's land, and it brought back with it a magnificent wild horse from the neighboring kingdom. When the neighbors saw the farmer's new acquisition, they came to congratulate him, saying, "How fortunate you are! Not only did your horse return, but it also brought you a splendid horse!"

Once again, the farmer replied with composure, "Maybe it's a blessing, maybe it's a curse. Who knows?"

As the farmer's son was trying to tame the wild horse, he fell off its back and broke his leg. The neighbors rushed to the farmer to express their sympathy, "What a terrible misfortune! Your son has broken his leg, and now he cannot help you with the farm work."

Yet again, the farmer's response was composed, "Maybe it's a blessing, maybe it's a curse. Who knows?" A short time later, the kingdom went to war with a neighboring state. All the young and able-bodied men were drafted into the army to fight, and many of them died in the battles. However, the farmer's son was spared from the conscription due to his broken leg.

The neighbors came to the farmer once more, amazed at how lucky he was that his son did not have to go to war, saying, "Your son's injury has saved his life! How fortunate you are!"

And once again, the farmer replied with his usual wisdom, "Maybe it's a blessing, maybe it's a curse. Who knows?"

The story of the lost horse reminds us that life is full of uncertainties, and what may seem like a misfortune at one moment can lead to unexpected blessings in the future, and vice versa. The farmer's attitude of equanimity teaches us the importance of accepting events with an open mind, without immediately labeling them as good or bad. It's a timeless lesson about the unpredictable nature of life and the need for humility in our judgments.

My failures allowed me the time to reflect on how the universe orchestrated my path precisely to where I needed to be. Amidst these failures, I experienced the most profound moment of gratitude. I am genuinely thankful for the opportunity that the Baltimore County Fire Department has given me. Being in this department led me to encounter a woman with a near-death experience, which ignited my spiritual journey My failures in the lieutenant and fire specialist exams served as the catalyst for finding the motivation to write this book.

This book marks the beginning of a new chapter in my life. My heart acknowledges that my time in this department has been fulfilled, having dedicated almost ten years to serving the citizens of Baltimore County. Now, I am embracing the calling to serve the world in a different capacity. Redirection in life can often be seen as a sign from the universe, guiding us toward our true growth and potential. These redirections can manifest in various forms, such as changes in job, scenery, or relationships. Although they may initially appear as challenges or obstacles, they often pave the way for greater personal and professional fulfillment. One of the most common forms of redirection occurs in our professional lives. We may find ourselves feeling stuck or unsatisfied in our current job despite our best efforts to make it work.

This feeling of stagnation can be disheartening, but it may also serve as a catalyst for change. The universe might be nudging us towards a new path, one that aligns more closely with our passions, talents, and purpose. It could be a whisper urging us to take a leap of faith and explore new opportunities that could unlock our true potential. Similarly, changes in scenery can provide a fresh perspective and serve as a powerful catalyst for personal growth. The universe might present us with opportunities to relocate, whether it's moving to a new city or country or even just exploring different environments within our current surroundings. These changes in scenery can help us break free from old patterns, step out of our comfort zones, and gain a broader understanding of ourselves and the world around us. They can ignite our creativity, broaden our horizons, and introduce us to new experiences and perspectives that nurture our personal growth. Relationships, too, can be subject to redirection. Sometimes, the universe guides us away from toxic or unfulfilling relationships that no longer serve our highest good. It may become evident that certain connections are hindering our personal growth and preventing us from reaching our true potential.

While these realizations can be challenging, they provide an opportunity to reflect, reassess our priorities, and seek relationships that align with our authentic selves. The universe may present new people, connections, or even the possibility of solitude to allow us to heal, grow, and thrive. Embracing redirection requires a willingness to listen to our intuition and to trust the signs the universe presents us. It may not always be easy or comfortable to let go of the familiar, but by doing so, we open ourselves up to new possibilities and allow our true potential to flourish. It is important to remember that redirection is not a punishment but rather a gentle nudge toward a more fulfilling and purposeful life.

In the face of redirection, it is crucial to remain open-minded and resilient. It may require patience, courage, and self-reflection to navigate these changes effectively. Trusting that the universe has our best interests at heart can help us overcome the fear and uncertainty that often accompany re-direction. By embracing the opportunities for growth and following the signs presented to us, we can embark on a transformative journey that leads us to a more authentic and fulfilling life. When life presents you with redirection in the form of a change in job, scenery, or relationship, take a moment to listen to the universe's message. Embrace the unknown, have faith in your own abilities, and embark on a journey of self-discovery and growth. The universe may be guiding you toward a path that will nurture your true potential.

CHAPTER ELEVEN

FLOWING WITH THE UNIVERSE

FLOWING WITH LIFE

One might think that writing a chapter about flowing with the universe would be incredibly easy. Believe it or not, when I reached that last chapter, I encountered writer's block; I didn't know where to begin with concluding this book. Consequently, I decided to take a solid month off from writing. During this time, my girlfriend Anastasia and I embarked on a few trips. Our first journey commenced in Mexico, where we visited Playa Del Carmen and Tulum.

At the start of the trip, I made a conscious decision not to dwell on the approaching deadline for the book. I was determined to enjoy the present moment fully. We had an amazing experience at an adult-only resort, with the highlight being the freedom to skinny dip in the pool whenever we wanted, along with savoring the incredible food. We felt extremely fortunate as every restaurant we chose served food that was nothing short of excellent.

One night, our anniversary dinner stood out the most. I had a desire for a Yin and Yang necklace to complete my outfit, and it felt like our night wouldn't have been complete without manifesting one. Remarkably, I ended up finding the perfect necklace, which I still wear to this day.

Following our Mexico trip, we impulsively decided to travel to Gatlinburg, Tennessee. I had prepared a list of things to do, but the universe had other plans for us. We both ended up getting food poisoning and as a result, we spent the first half of the trip confined to our cabin. However, despite not doing much, we cherished the time we spent together. We danced to music and sat on the back porch, listening to the soothing sound of the water flowing from the stream behind our cabin. It was a peaceful and serene experience. Our mindset shifted during this trip as we let go of expectations and allowed whatever happened to happen. The next day, we ventured into town, only to discover that finding parking was extremely difficult due to the holiday rush. Initially, I had planned to have breakfast at Pancake Pantry, but the impossibly long line discouraged us, and we were starving.

Fortunately, Anastasia spotted a rooftop Mexican restaurant and immediately expressed her desire to eat there. Although I wasn't particularly in the mood for lunch, and Mexican food wasn't my first choice, I decided not to resist her judgment. Looking back, I'm glad I went along because the food and drinks turned out to be amazing. However, we were still cautious after recovering from food poisoning and didn't want to overindulge. The last thing we wanted was to experience digestive issues in a public restroom. Hence, I decided to head back after the satisfying meal.

As we made our way back to the car, we noticed a booth offering tours and activities for Gatlinburg. We were specifically interested in learning more about the Anakeesta Mountaintop park. An elderly gentleman at the booth provided us with the information we sought and then playfully inquired about our age. Amused by his remark, he said, "I thought you guys were a lot younger, but now that I know you're older than I thought, you can get free money to do these activities! However, you have to attend a 90-minute presentation for the Westgate resort." Now, I should mention that I have the option to stay in Gatlinburg for free with the campground where I work part-time, so the prospect of a timeshare didn't appeal to me much. Nevertheless, the gentleman offered us $120 if we were willing to spend two hours listening to their sales pitch. That piqued my interest, as he had my attention at the mention of free money.

He guided us across the street to take us to the resort, and we patiently sat through the presentation. Once it was over, the salesman offered to give us a tour of the resort, but since we had already exceeded the promised 90 minutes, I asked if we could skip it. The salesperson agreed and consulted with his supervisors. After a brief absence, the supervisor approached us with the check to take to the bank. We felt a bit sorry for the young college student because the supervisors seemed tough on him for not making a deal.

When we were done, we returned to our car and waited for the transport shuttle to take us back downtown. Interestingly, the same man who had transported us to the resort was our driver again. However, this time, he took the scenic route back to town. During the ride, he gave us a mini tour, showing us the top of the skywalk, and to our surprise, we even encountered a Black bear. People around us stopped their cars to take pictures, but we assumed bear sightings were normal, considering they appeared on every form of merchandise in Gatlinburg. Our driver informed us that bears had become rare in town because they were working to keep them away. He mentioned that in his 26 years of living there, it was only his third bear sighting, emphasizing how lucky we were to stumble across one.

Upon finally reaching our car, we felt genuinely grateful for the unexpected bear encounter and the free money we received. Our initial plan was to return to town later that night to witness the pre-4th of July parade, as Gatlinburg took pride in having the first parade at midnight. However, as we returned to the cabin, Anastasia and I mutually decided to stay in for the night and simply enjoy the cabin. Surprisingly, none of our Fear of Missing Out (FOMO) instincts kicked in. We both instinctively knew to stay put and regroup for the festivities planned for the following day.

The next day, feeling much better, we decided to use the free money we received to go water tubing. The weather and water conditions were perfect, setting the stage for a wonderful day ahead. While tubing, Anastasia and I found ourselves drifting towards the sides of the river, which caused us to stop moving with the flow of the water. In an attempt to prevent this, I searched for a stick to steer us away from the sides. I found a small stick nearby, which led to a light-hearted comment from an older gentleman floating nearby. "That's some stick you get there."

Playfully responding to his remark, I tossed the small stick aside and found a larger one. Observing the gentleman just relaxing and effortlessly going with the river's current, I saw it as a sign from the universe. He demonstrated how to naturally go with the flow and encounter no resistance. Inspired by this, we released our worries about getting stuck and allowed ourselves to be carried along with the water. From then on, our journey became smooth and enjoyable.

Later that night, Anastasia expressed worry about missing the fireworks, assuming they were only happening in Pigeon Forge. However, I assured her that I had planned a memorable 4th of July for her and asked her to trust me. To help calm her anxiety, I took her to get some pizza, and the people there also supported our decision to head to Anakeesta for the fireworks. After savoring our pizza, we made our way to the Anakeesta lift. It treated us to a stunning nighttime skyline view of Gatlinburg, accompanied by beautiful fireworks from the ski lift.

The scene was exactly as I had envisioned, and I felt grateful for not giving in to her anxiety and choosing Pigeon Forge instead. We had the best view anyone could ask for, and the line of people waiting to go down the ski lift only reaffirmed that we had made the right choice.

Once at the top of Anakeesta, we continued watching the fireworks before heading over to Astra Lumina, an enchanting night walk under the stars that added the perfect touch to our night. As we danced under the stars, I reflected on how the universe had allowed us to flow with it.

These trips provided me with the inspiration to commence this chapter. Surprisingly, it was the act of doing absolutely nothing related to the book that led to these profound experiences and formed the introduction to this chapter. In the context of Daoism, this can be described as being in harmony with the Dao, aligning one's actions with the natural laws of the universe. When we flow with the Dao, we effortlessly find ourselves in the right place at the right time–this is known as Wu-Wei.

OVERSTANDING TAOISM

In order to grasp Wu-Wei, we have to have a better understanding of where the concept originates from. It wouldn't be right to create a chapter about flowing with the universe if we didn't address Taoism. I'm sure some of you noticed earlier in the chapter, we used "Daoism" as opposed to "Taoism".

The spelling with a T and D is a result of the transliteration of the Chinese word "道教" (pronounced as "Dàojiào") into English. The Chinese language has a different phonetic system than English. When translating Chinese words into English, there is often no direct one-to-one mapping of sounds.

In the Wade-Giles system, which was historically used for transliterating Chinese into English, the Chinese character "道"

was transliterated as "Tao," and the character "教" was transliterated as "Chiao." Hence, the religion or philosophy that follows the teachings of "道" (Tao) became known as "Taoism." However, the Wade-Giles system has largely been replaced by the Pinyin system, which is the current standard for transliterating Chinese into English. In Pinyin, the same Chinese word "道教" is transliterated as "Daojiao." Therefore, according to modern Pinyin standards, the term would be spelled "Daoism" instead of "Taoism."

Despite the more accurate Pinyin transliteration, the term "Taoism" has been widely used and recognized in English-speaking countries for a long time, and thus it remains prevalent today. In order to prevent further confusion, we will be using the Wade-Giles system.

KEY CONCEPTS AND PRINCIPLES OF TAOISM

Taoism is an ancient Chinese philosophical and spiritual tradition that dates back over two millennia. It is based on the foundational text, the "Tao Te Ching," attributed to the legendary sage Laozi (Lao Tzu), although the exact origins of Taoism are shrouded in mystery and folklore. Taoism focuses on living in harmony with the Tao, which can be translated as "The way" or "The path."

The Tao is one of the most essential and profound aspects of Taoist thought. The word "Tao" can be translated in various ways, including "The way," "The path," "The way of nature," or "The ultimate reality." However, it is important to note that the Tao transcends precise definition and is difficult to fully express in words. The Tao is considered formless and beyond conceptual understanding. It cannot be adequately described or defined in language because it is the source from which all things arise, including language itself.

Taoists believe that the Tao is the origin of everything that exists in the universe. It is the underlying principle that governs the natural order of creation and guides all processes and changes. The Tao is both immanent and transcendent, encompassing all dualities and contradictions. It embraces the principles of Yin and Yang, representing the dynamic interplay of complementary forces in the world.

The Tao represents the inherent order and harmony of the universe. It is the natural rhythm and flow that governs all phenomena and leads to spontaneous, balanced actions.

The Tao does not favor one thing over another. It is impartial and does not judge or differentiate between good and bad, right and wrong. It allows things to be as they are without interference. Following the Tao is a path to wisdom and virtue. By aligning oneself with the natural order and living in harmony with the Tao, individuals can cultivate inner peace, compassion, and a sense of interconnectedness with all life.

Taoism teaches that returning to the Tao, the ultimate source, is the ultimate goal. This can be achieved through spiritual practices, self-cultivation, and letting go of attachments and desires.

Wu-Wei (无为)

The concept of "Non-action," "Effortless action," or "Actionless action." It is a state of being in which one acts effortlessly and spontaneously, in perfect harmony with the natural flow of events. It refers to the practice of aligning oneself with the natural flow of the Dao (Tao) and achieving harmony by acting in a spontaneous and effortless manner without unnecessary interference or striving.

The term may seem contradictory since it suggests that one achieves success or harmony by not actively doing anything. However, the essence of Wu-Wei lies in the natural flow and spontaneity of actions rather than forced or contrived efforts. It is about aligning oneself with the natural course of events and allowing things to unfold organically without unnecessary resistance.

Wu-Wei is often likened to the way water flows effortlessly, following the path of least resistance. It does not imply inactivity or laziness but rather involves acting in harmony with the underlying principles of nature. By doing so, one can achieve greater effectiveness and efficiency in their actions. The central idea behind Wu-Wei is that by letting go of excessive striving, personal desires, and ego-driven actions, one can achieve a state of greater effectiveness and tranquility. It is not about inaction or laziness but rather about aligning oneself with the natural order of things and acting in accordance with it.

In the context of Wu-Wei, action is considered effortless when it is free from unnecessary effort, resistance, or coercion. It is about being in a state of flow, where actions arise naturally and effortlessly without the need for conscious planning or forceful exertion.

Wu-Wei is often associated with spontaneity, intuition, and mindfulness. It involves being fully present in the current moment without being attached to outcomes or preoccupied with the past or future. By cultivating a state of Wu-Wei, individuals can tap into their inner wisdom and respond to situations with greater clarity and effectiveness.

This concept can be applied to various aspects of life, including personal relationships, work, and creative pursuits. It suggests that by letting go of rigid expectations and striving for control, one can create space for unexpected possibilities and allow things to unfold naturally.

One excellent example of Wu-Wei can be found in Chapter 48 of the Dao De Jing:

> "In the pursuit of learning, every day something is acquired.
> In the pursuit of the Tao, every day something is dropped.
> Less and less is done
> Until non-action is achieved.
> When nothing is done, nothing is left undone.
> It cannot be ruled by interfering.
> The Sage does not accumulate anything
> Yet the more he does for others, the more he has.
> The more he gives to others, the greater his abundance."

In this passage, Laozi emphasizes the principle of Wu-Wei by contrasting it with the pursuit of conventional knowledge and ambition. The pursuit of learning involves acquiring knowledge and accumulating things, while the pursuit of the Tao involves letting go and simplifying one's actions.

The Tao cultivator refrains from excessive interference and control. Instead of forcefully trying to impose their will on the world, they allow events to unfold naturally, like water flowing without resistance. By doing less and dropping unnecessary desires, the Tao practitioner achieves a state of effortlessness. They don't strive for results, but instead, they let things manifest naturally. The Sage, the enlightened one who embodies Wu-Wei, is not concerned with accumulating possessions or seeking personal gain. Yet, the more they give and act in a selfless manner, the more abundance and virtue they cultivate. This example from the Tao Te Ching demonstrates the profound wisdom of Wu-Wei, encouraging individuals to embrace simplicity, act in harmony with the natural order, and find greater fulfillment through selfless actions and letting go of excessive desires.

☯ YIN AND YANG ☯

The Yin and Yang symbol is something that many people may have come across without giving it much thought. I used to see it often but didn't pay much attention, considering it merely a simple Chinese symbol. However, everything changed when I met Anastasia.

Anastasia was the one who made me notice the symbol whenever we encountered it. Whether on a shirt, tattoo, or bumper sticker, she would always spot it. What intrigued us was that every time we noticed it, something positive would happen in our lives. This recurring pattern led us to believe that it was a sign from the universe, guiding us in the right direction.

One particular night, we attended a Dru Hill concert in Washington, DC. Among the crowd, there was an intoxicated man who initially irritated us by cutting in line. Later, he approached us and said, "I don't know what's making me say this, but something tells me to tell you both not to stop what you're doing. I feel your light and energy, and I love it. Keep it up." Curious, Anastasia pointed out the Yin and Yang symbols on his hoodie. He said what he had to say, then disappeared for the rest of the night.

We interpreted this encounter as a defining moment in our relationship, seeing this man as a conduit of the universe. It reminded us that our journey together was divinely guided. Though our relationship faced ups and downs, the presence of the Yin and Yang symbol and the positive messages we received served as reassuring signs that we would be okay. Who would have thought that such a seemingly simple symbol carried so much wisdom? Understanding its meaning has given us a deeper appreciation for the ups and downs of life itself.

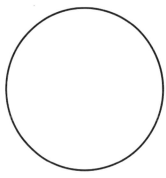

First, we have to break down the symbol itself. The concept of Yin and Yang is said to be embedded in **Wuji (无极)**: Wuji refers to the state of "Ultimate emptiness" or "Absolute nothingness." In Taoist cosmology, the universe is believed to have originated from this state of Wuji. From Wuji, the dualistic principles of Yin and Yang emerge, giving rise to all things in existence. In this sense, Wuji represents the pre-existing state of the cosmos before creation.

Taiji (太極): Often referred to as the "Great ultimate" or the "Supreme ultimate," emerges from Wuji. It is the state of duality or polarity where differentiation begins to arise from the undifferentiated state of Wuji. Taiji is depicted as a circle divided into two halves — one white and one black—representing the interaction of Yin and Yang, the dual forces that give rise to all existence.

White Half (Yang)

Black Half (Yin)

- Yin represents the dark, shadowy, and hidden aspects of life.
- It is often associated with feminine energy and characteristics.
- Yin is passive, receptive, and nurturing.
- It is connected to coldness and coolness.
- Yin is related to the earth and its grounding qualities.
- Yin is associated with the moon and its cycles.

White Half (Yang)

- Yang represents light, brightness, and illumination.
- It is often associated with masculine energy and characteristics.
- Yang is active, assertive, and dynamic.
- It is connected to warmth and heat.
- Yang is related to the heavens and the celestial realms.
- Yang is associated with the sun and its energy.

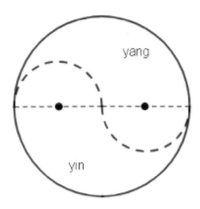

The boundary between the black and white halves takes the form of a sinuous line, forming an s-curve. This curve indicates the dynamic and cyclical nature of the interplay between Yin and Yang. Within each half, there is a smaller dot of the opposite color. These dots symbolize the idea that within Yin, there is a seed of Yang, and within Yang, there is a seed of Yin. This reflects the concept of interconnectedness and the continuous interplay between the two forces.

Imagine a pendulum swinging back and forth. As it reaches its highest point, it briefly pauses before changing direction and starts swinging back in the opposite direction. Similarly, in life and various processes, when something reaches its peak or extreme, it tends to transform into its polar opposite.

For instance, consider the economy. During a period of rapid economic growth, we often witness soaring stock markets, high consumer spending, and low unemployment rates. However, when the economy reaches its peak, it may suddenly start to slow down, leading to a downturn or recession. The robust expansion transforms into its opposite, a contraction. Another example could be the weather. The changing seasons serve as a profound analogy for the Yin and Yang cycle of change. Spring (Yang to Yin transition):

Spring marks the beginning of the cycle when Yang's energy starts to rise. The days become longer, temperatures increase, and nature awakens with new growth. As the Yang energy reaches its peak during late spring, it transforms into its opposite, Yin.

Summer represents the height of Yang energy, with its long, hot days and flourishing vegetation. However, as summer reaches its peak, it starts to wane, and the days gradually become shorter. The transition from summer to autumn signifies the transformation of Yang into Yin. During autumn, the Yang energy diminishes, and the weather cools down. Leaves fall from the trees, and nature prepares for dormancy. As autumn reaches its peak, it transforms into Yin, setting the stage for the upcoming season.

Winter embodies the depth of Yin energy with its short, cold days and barren landscapes. However, as the winter solstice passes, Yin energy starts to wane, and the days gradually become longer. Winter, at its peak transforms into Yang, heralding the arrival of spring and initiating the cycle anew.

The changing seasons beautifully illustrate the cyclical nature of the Yin and Yang cycle, where the energy of each season reaches its zenith before transforming into its polar opposite. This pattern of change and transformation is fundamental in various aspects of life, reflecting the interconnectedness and harmony of opposing forces.

Balancing Dualities

The Yin and Yang symbol illustrates the harmonious interplay and balance between two complementary forces. Everything in the universe consists of these dualistic qualities, and they are in a constant state of flux and transformation. They are not opposing forces but rather two aspects of the same whole, representing the cyclical nature of existence.

The symbol implies that nothing is purely Yin or purely Yang; rather, everything contains elements of both, and their proportions may vary. Achieving balance between Yin and Yang is considered essential for harmony and well-being in various aspects of life, including health, relationships, and the environment. Growing up, I was a massive Star Wars fan, to the extent that I dedicated an entire tattoo sleeve to the dark side of the Force. In my personal opinion, I always believed that they had cooler powers, but that's beside the point. Looking at the philosophical aspect of Star Wars, one can easily draw parallels between the fundamental principles in both the Star Wars universe and the ancient Chinese philosophy.

The most obvious connection between Star Wars and Yin and Yang is the theme of balance. In the Star Wars saga, the Force represents a cosmic energy that has both light and dark sides. The Jedi embody the light side, while the Sith embrace the dark side. The concept of balance is prevalent throughout the series, with characters like Anakin Skywalker/Darth Vader and Rey seeking to bring harmony to the Force by reconciling both aspects within themselves.

The light and dark sides of the Force in Star Wars rely on each other for their existence. Without darkness, there would be no light, and vice versa. This interdependence is exemplified by the ongoing struggle between the Jedi and the Sith, where one cannot exist without the other.

Many characters in Star Wars reflect the duality of Yin and Yang within themselves. Anakin Skywalker, for instance, embodies both light and dark qualities, ultimately leading him to become both a heroic Jedi Knight and a feared Sith Lord. Characters like Luke Skywalker and Rey also grapple with their internal conflicts, trying to find a balance between their altruistic impulses and their darker emotions.

The struggle between the light and dark sides of the Force in Star Wars mirrors the ethical choices individuals face in life. It emphasizes the importance of making conscious decisions to maintain balance and harmony, as depicted in the philosophy of Yin and Yang.

In Star Wars, the galaxy experiences periods of harmony and peace when balance is maintained in the force, but it also faces conflict and turmoil when the balance is disrupted. This cyclic nature of balance and conflict is reminiscent of the Yin and Yang symbol's dynamic movement.

Yin and Yang symbolize the constant process of change and transformation. This aspect is well-reflected in the personal growth and development of characters in Star Wars. Many characters undergo transformative journeys, changing from one side of the Force to the other or finding their own path to balance.

Overall, Star Wars' exploration of the force and its connection to the concepts of Yin and Yang adds depth and philosophical richness to the epic saga, making it more than just a classic tale of good versus evil. It illustrates the complexity of human nature and the ongoing quest for harmony and balance in a universe where opposing forces perpetually coexist.

We must embrace both the divine feminine (Yin) and the divine masculine (Yang) energy. An imbalance of Yin energy can lead to various health and emotional issues. When Yin energy dominates a person or situation, it can lead to excessive passivity and lack of initiative. This might result in missed opportunities, stagnation, and an unwillingness to take necessary actions.

On the emotional spectrum, an imbalance of Yin energy may lead to feelings of sadness, depression, and hopelessness. This is often associated with the dark, cold, and introspective nature of Yin. Yin energy is often linked to coldness, both in a physical and emotional sense. In relationships, too much Yin can lead to emotional withdrawal and a lack of warmth and intimacy.

The dark side of Yin can cause individuals to isolate themselves from others, leading to feelings of loneliness and disconnectedness. When Yin energy is misused or not balanced with Yang, it can manifest as manipulative behavior or passive-aggressiveness. While sensitivity is not inherently negative, too much Yin energy can lead to hypersensitivity, making individuals overly reactive to criticism or perceived slights. A predominantly Yin-oriented individual might struggle with assertiveness, finding it difficult to stand up for themselves or voice their needs and desires. The dark side of Yin can cause a person to rely excessively on others for support and decision-making, leading to a lack of independence and self-reliance.

Instead of facing challenges and responsibilities, individuals dominated by Yin energy might resort to escapism through various means, such as excessive daydreaming, substance abuse, or overindulgence in entertainment.

This imbalance manifests in our physical health in various ways. Excessive Yin energy can lead to feelings of fatigue and lethargy. People may lack motivation and find it challenging to muster the energy to engage in activities. People with an excess of Yin energy may feel excessively sensitive to cold weather and have difficulty staying warm, even in moderate temperatures. Imbalanced Yin energy can cause water retention in the body, leading to swelling, particularly in the extremities. A Yin imbalance can lead to a slow pulse rate and a sluggish metabolism, affecting overall vitality and digestion.

Imbalanced Yin energy can lead to a lack of creativity, enthusiasm, and passion in life. It may feel like life has lost its luster. In women, Yin imbalance can lead to menstrual irregularities, such as heavy or prolonged periods or even the absence of menstruation.

On the other end of the spectrum, just like an imbalance of Yin energy, an imbalance of Yang energy can also lead to various health and emotional issues. Yang is the counterpart to Yin and represents qualities such as light, activity, heat, masculinity, and the sun. Like Yin, Yang is not inherently negative, but it can have a dark side when taken to extremes or when imbalanced. Here are some ways the dark side of yang can manifest. An excessive amount of Yang energy can lead to aggressive and violent behavior. This can manifest in personal relationships, in societal interactions, or on a larger geopolitical scale. If we understand "Yang energy" in the context of excessive dominance, aggression, or assertiveness in leadership, some historical leaders have been described as possessing such traits. Adolf Hitler's leadership style could be seen as embodying excessive Yang energy. His pursuit of absolute power, aggressive expansionism, and authoritarian tendencies reflect an overwhelming dominance and a lack of balance with more peaceful and nurturing aspects.

The dark side of Yang may result in a desire for dominance and control over others, leading to oppressive and authoritarian behavior. Too much Yang energy can create a sense of restlessness and impatience, making it challenging to relax, be patient, and practice mindfulness.

When Yang's energy is not tempered with humility, it can lead to arrogance and an inflated sense of Self-importance. An excess of Yang energy can lead to a single-minded focus on goals and objectives, potentially disregarding other important aspects of life.

An overly Yang-oriented person might be less attuned to the emotional needs and feelings of others, leading to a lack of empathy and understanding. The dark side of Yang can result in impulsive and reckless behavior without proper consideration of consequences. While healthy competition can be motivating, an excessive Yang focus on winning and outperforming others can lead to a cutthroat and unhealthy competitive mindset. Yang energy, when imbalanced, may prioritize material success and achievements over personal well-being and meaningful connections.

As far as our physical health goes, excessive Yang energy can lead to feelings of restlessness, nervousness, and agitation. Too much Yang energy can disrupt the balance needed for restful sleep, leading to insomnia and other sleep disturbances. Falling asleep and staying asleep may become difficult.

People may find it challenging to relax and experience a constant sense of hyperactivity. An excess of Yang energy can affect the digestive system, leading to symptoms like acid reflux, heartburn, and excessive hunger. It may also cause an increase in bowel movements or diarrhea.

Yang energy imbalance can lead to an increase in blood pressure and a rapid or irregular pulse rate. This can put additional strain on the cardiovascular system. People experiencing an imbalance of Yang energy may be overly sensitive to heat. They might feel hot even in moderate temperatures or have a tendency to sweat excessively.

Recognizing an imbalance of Yin and Yang energy within ourselves is crucial for maintaining overall well-being and leading a harmonious life. We must maintain the equilibrium between Yin and Yang that allows for a clear and focused mind. By balancing these energies, we can achieve mental clarity and make better decisions.

When Yin and Yang are in harmony, we experience a sense of inner peace and contentment. Our mind is not overly dominated by extreme emotions or racing thoughts, leading to a state of mental tranquility. The balance of Yin and Yang is believed to support overall well-being, strengthen the body, and prevent illness.

Yin and Yang are associated with the flow of vital energy (Qi) in the body. When the energies are balanced, Qi can flow smoothly through the meridians, ensuring proper nourishment to different organs and tissues. This helps to enhance vitality and prevent energy blockages that might lead to health issues. A balanced Yin and Yang are thought to strengthen the immune system, making the body more resilient to external pathogens. The immune system's balance relies on the harmonious interaction of opposing forces, just like Yin and Yang.

To enhance the balance of Yin and Yang and improve mental and physical health, individuals can engage in practices such as Tai Chi, Qi Gong, and meditation. These activities aim to harmonize the body's energies, promote relaxation, and foster a deeper connection with the natural rhythms of the universe.

LIVING IN ALIGNMENT WITH THE TAO

As we conclude this book, I wanted to share a few lessons from Lao Tzu that have had a profound impact on my life. The first is "When you look within, you find everything you need." Lao Tzu suggests that all the answers and resources one needs are not external but can be found by introspection and looking within oneself. It emphasizes the significance of self-discovery and self-reliance as opposed to seeking solutions solely from external sources.

The quote implies that there is a wellspring of wisdom, knowledge, and understanding within each individual. By turning our attention inward, we can access this inherent wisdom and gain insights into our lives, challenges, and purpose.

Recognizing that everything one needs is already within promotes a sense of contentment with what one has and reduces the constant pursuit of external desires. The quote suggests that the present moment contains everything one needs. By being fully present and attentive to the now, individuals can tap into their inner resources and deal with whatever arises in a more centered and composed manner.

The resonance I personally felt with this experience stemmed from my past tendency to seek external validation. After ending a nine and a half-year relationship, I found myself grappling with a sense of emptiness. For so long, I had grown accustomed to having someone by my side that I couldn't comprehend what it meant to be alone. Interestingly, around the time of the breakup, a photo of mine unexpectedly went viral on social media, catapulting me into a modeling career. The sudden surge of attention inflated my ego, and I became fixated on my image and the admiration I received from women online. I developed a compulsion to take constant selfies, craving that immediate gratification. My ego started controlling me, and I began to believe that I could easily win over any woman I desired. In an attempt to fill the void within me, I sought the company of multiple women, thinking it would satisfy my emotional needs. However, I soon realized that this pursuit left me unfulfilled and discontented. As time passed, I noticed something unexpected–I genuinely enjoyed the freedom of being unattached, without anyone to answer to or any relationship constraints.

This realization marked a significant lesson in my journey, drawing me closer to the teachings of Lao Tzu. It made me reflect on the importance of inner contentment and the value of being comfortable with oneself, even in solitude.

Change is inevitable, so embrace it.

During my various encounters with women, I had the privilege of meeting Anastasia, and right from the start, I sensed that she was unlike anyone else. I likened her to soul food, while the others felt like mere junk food, leaving me unsatisfied and empty afterward. It almost felt as if some higher force had guided her into my life. Despite recognizing her uniqueness, my ego still held sway over me, and I wasn't prepared to relinquish my freedom. The initial stages of our relationship were filled with turbulence and resistance because I resisted embracing change.

Anastasia's presence came at a time when I had an imbalance of both masculine and feminine energies within me. Wounded masculine energy often clings to success, seeks to be always right, acts selfishly aggressively, and remains disconnected from emotions. On the other hand, wounded feminine energy may seek external validation, display insecurities, manipulation, and a desperate need for love.

Anastasia fearlessly called me out on all these traits, questioning why I spent so much time with women and hardly ever with male friends. My ego resisted accepting her observations, as it meant acknowledging that I relied on women to validate myself because I couldn't validate myself.

Anastasia embodied an awakened masculine energy, one that confronts everything with unyielding clarity. They see through facades, recognizing when you're not being genuine with yourself and others. Their grounding and awareness bring to light all the hidden or denied aspects of yourself. Encountering someone with awakened masculine energy pushes you toward your higher self, but it requires being receptive to having your ego checked. I had to learn that it was entirely acceptable for a woman to embody the divine masculine. Both divine masculine and divine feminine energies exist within each of us, and they need to be balanced, akin to the concept of Yin and Yang. When a woman has already embraced this state, she can elevate those she encounters, as Anastasia did for me. From the very beginning, she asserted, "I always make the men in my life better," and she fulfilled that statement. Our encounter was meant to elevate my energy, but for that to happen, I had to embrace change wholeheartedly.

Change is an inherent and unavoidable aspect of existence. Nothing in the world remains stagnant; everything is subject to continuous transformation, whether on a personal, societal, or cosmic level. It is a fundamental law of nature that things are in a constant state of flux.

Rather than resisting or fearing change, Lao Tzu advises embracing it. This mindset suggests that by accepting change and flowing with it, we can adapt more effectively to new circumstances. Resisting change can lead to suffering and unnecessary struggles, as it goes against the natural course of life.

The concept of embracing change aligns with the Buddhist principle of impermanence (anicca). It teaches us that everything is temporary, and clinging to things or situations only leads to attachment and suffering. By embracing the impermanence of life, we can find greater peace and contentment. Embracing change requires flexibility and resilience. When we are open to change, we are better equipped to handle life's uncertainties and challenges. It allows us to let go of rigid expectations and adapt to new circumstances with grace. Embracing change can lead to personal growth and self-improvement. Change often presents opportunities for learning, self-discovery, and development. By being receptive to change, we can discover new possibilities and paths in our lives.

Letting go of your labels if you truly want to know yourself.

Anastasia's unique perspective became evident right from the beginning, as she remained unimpressed by my role as a firefighter or my massive social media following. Surprisingly, she didn't even have any social media accounts herself, highlighting our opposing views on this platform.

Her perspective challenged me to reevaluate my own relationship with social media. I began to see how the constant display of happiness and glamour on social media didn't necessarily reflect true happiness behind closed doors. People glorifying their vacations weren't fully experiencing the moment; instead, they were preoccupied with documenting every second. This introspection led me to question my own actions–I realized I, too, was seeking validation through my posts. I pondered, "Who am I trying to prove something to?" Unable to find a meaningful answer, I recognized that it was my ego seeking this self-validation, attaching itself to worldly accolades like being a firefighter, a model, or a social media influencer. But in truth, I am more than these labels—I am simply me, interconnected with all things as part of the universe.

With this realization, I understood that my achievements and accolades don't define me, as none of them truly matters in the grand scheme of things. Consequently, I took a decisive step—I deleted all modeling-related content in every selfie I had ever taken and disconnected from every woman with whom I had romantic involvement while under the influence of my ego.

This act symbolized my decision to "(E)dge (G)od) (O)ut" of my identity, shedding the limitations of labels. This transformation allowed the universe to flow through me freely. I discovered that the universe had a greater purpose for me—a mission to shift the collective consciousness of humanity.

The turning point came when I stopped rigidly defining myself by these superficial aspects, realizing that my true essence transcends these temporary identifications. By letting go of the ego's grasp, I opened myself up to the universe's guidance, which moved through me in a profound and transformative way.

"He who defines himself can't know who he really is. He who has power over others can't empower himself." **Lao Tzu, Tao Te Chin**

Lao Tzu emphasizes the importance of letting go of the labels and preconceived notions that society and others may place on us. These labels can include job titles, social status, cultural affiliations, and even personality traits that we believe define us.

By identifying ourselves solely with these labels, we limit our understanding of who we truly are at a deeper level. True self-awareness requires peeling back these superficial layers to reach the core of our being. It involves looking inward and acknowledging our thoughts, emotions, desires, strengths, and weaknesses without the influence of external definitions. When we release attachments to labels, we free ourselves from the limitations they impose. We open the door to self-discovery, enabling a deeper understanding of our authentic selves. Embracing this idea can lead to greater self-acceptance, self-compassion, and a more profound connection with our true essence. "Embrace simplicity"

Last year, Anastasia and I made a joint decision to step outside our comfort zone and trust our intuition. We faced a choice between renewing our overpriced lease in Tyson's Corner, Virginia or investing that money in an RV to embrace a nomadic lifestyle. After carefully weighing the pros and cons, we ultimately chose the adventurous path of RV living.

As a child, I had a deep desire to live in an RV, and the joy I felt whenever my dad took me to a mobile home park was unmatched. His playful prediction that I would one day live in an RV park stayed with me, almost like he had planted the seed of this dream long ago. Looking back, it feels like he unwittingly manifested this path for me, setting the stage for my RV lifestyle today.

Anastasia discovered a 2021 Forest River Vibe, though initially, I resisted, longing for a larger 5th wheel. Yet, the universe had other plans, and once we set foot in the Vibe, both of us felt an immediate sense of belonging. Everything seemed to fall into place afterward.

In the initial month, I landed a part-time maintenance role at the campground, which might come as a surprise to some, considering my background as a firefighter. However, I discovered immense satisfaction in repairing and mastering tasks with my hands rather than dealing with emergencies. It felt like I was fulfilling a soul contract as if I was reconnecting with skills from a previous life. Gradually, I honed my abilities and gained confidence in handling electrical and plumbing challenges, expanding my skill set beyond what I had imagined. Living and working amidst nature has nurtured compassion within me towards the environment. I've come to acknowledge the profound interconnectedness between all living beings and the natural world, harmoniously flowing with the Tao. A remarkable encounter with a wolf spider reinforced this awareness. When the spider landed on my arm, instead of reacting with fear, I found a sense of calm within me. I recognized the spider not as a mere pest but as a fellow being with whom I share a profound connection. This newfound perspective has enriched my experiences in the great outdoors, fostering a deeper appreciation for the beauty and harmony of the natural world.

The opportunity to work and camp has granted me grounding experiences and deep gratitude. Our stress-free and simple life frees us from worrying about expensive rent in Tyson's Corner, and instead, the money we save goes towards enriching our lives through travel and shared memories. This lifestyle has taught us to find joy in the simple things and cherish every moment. As we embrace this way of living, I've come to realize that true wealth lies in the abundance of joy, love, and meaningful experiences rather than material possessions. My journey has taught me patience in dealing with adversities, and I am grateful for the growth it has brought into my life. Through this new lifestyle, we've unlocked a sense of eternal wealth and contentment, cherishing the journey and the valuable lessons it brings.

"Simplicity, patience, compassion. These three are your greatest treasures." **Tao Te Ching, Chapter 67.**

This quote alone encapsulates fundamental principles and the importance of living a harmonious and balanced life. Simplicity refers to living a life that is uncomplicated and free from unnecessary complexities. Embracing simplicity means letting go of excessive desires, material possessions, and superficial pursuits. By simplifying our lives, we can focus on what truly matters, find contentment in the present moment and appreciate the natural flow of life. Patience is a virtue that allows individuals to endure difficulties and challenges with a calm and composed demeanor. Patience involves embracing the ebb and flow of life without resistance. Practicing patience means allowing events to unfold naturally without forcing outcomes or trying to control the uncontrollable. By cultivating compassion, individuals develop a sense of interconnectedness with all living beings, leading to a more harmonious existence and fostering a sense of unity with the world.

Together, these three treasures form a foundation for living a balanced and fulfilling life according to Taoist principles. Embracing simplicity helps individuals find contentment and reduce unnecessary stress and distractions. Patience allows individuals to navigate the ups and downs of life with grace, avoiding impulsive actions or reactions. Compassion fosters a sense of community and harmony, promoting a deeper understanding of others and oneself.

Embrace the silence.

"Silence is a source of strength," **Lao Tzu.**

The last lesson I want to leave you all with is the strength of silence. Silence is often viewed as a negative or an absence of something; however, in Taoism, it is viewed as a great strength. In today's fast-paced world with constant notifications, information overload, and sensory bombardment, finding moments of silence can be liberating.

It offers respite from overstimulation and allows us to recharge our minds and bodies. Embracing silence implies finding stillness and tranquility in one's surroundings and within oneself. In the busy and chaotic world we live in, taking moments of silence allows us to reflect, contemplate, and gain clarity about our thoughts, feelings, and actions.

Silence can be an avenue to inner peace. When we silence the noise around us and the mental chatter within, we open ourselves to better understanding our true nature and the essence of existence. Embracing silence also involves becoming a better listener. By being silent, we allow ourselves to truly listen to others and comprehend their perspectives. It fosters empathy, compassion, and a deeper understanding of the people and the world around us.

Embracing silence can be seen as connecting with the natural world and observing its quiet rhythms. Spending time in nature and appreciating its silence can lead to a sense of harmony and oneness with the universe. Silence can be a fertile ground for creativity and intuition. It gives space for new ideas to emerge and helps us tap into our subconscious mind.

"Without going out of the door, one can know the world. Without looking out of the window, one can see the Tao of Heaven. The further one goes, the less one knows." **Tao Te Ching, Chapter 47**

The verse suggests that you don't necessarily need to travel or seek external knowledge to understand the nature of existence. Instead, by turning inward and cultivating inner stillness, you can gain a deeper understanding of the world and its underlying principles. By embracing silence and refraining from constant external distractions, one can develop clarity and wisdom. This quiet observation of the world allows us to perceive the subtleties and truths that might go unnoticed in the busyness of life. It encourages a more profound connection with the essence of existence and the underlying harmony of the universe.

Silence is the gateway to your intuition and higher guidance. When the mind is still, you are more receptive to intuitive insights and messages from your higher self. These insights often arise as subtle nudges, gut feelings, or a sense of knowing that comes from a deeper level of consciousness.

Silence allows you to align with higher frequencies or spiritual energies. By attuning yourself to these elevated vibrations, you can elevate your own consciousness and connect to your higher self. The ego tends to dominate our thoughts and actions, clouding the connection to our higher self. Silence can help transcend these egoic patterns and detach from the identification with external Factors. In this state, you can experience a greater sense of unity and oneness with the higher aspects of your being.

It's through the profound stillness of introspection when the clamor of the mind subsides, and the soul embraces serenity, the universe reveals its ethereal voice. It whispers ancient truths and cosmic secrets, resonating through the very fabric of existence. The celestial symphony unfolds before the receptive heart as the dance of stars illuminates the pathways of enlightenment. In the sacred communion of silence, we become attuned to the harmonious cadence of creation, where the universe speaks in a language beyond words, weaving an eternal bond between the seeker and the cosmos, forever guiding us toward the luminous essence of our being. The universe speaks when one is silent enough to listen to the cosmic whisper.

Sources

Chapter 1

- Being, O. (2019). Symbols of Power: Adinkras and the Nature of reality. *The on Being Project.* https://onbeing.org/blog/symbols-of-power-adinkras-and-the-nature-of-reality/
- *Jim Gates and the symmetry of space and time | American Association for the Advancement of Science (AAAS).* (n.d.). American Association for the Advancement of Science (AAAS). https://www.aaas.org/jim-gates-and-symmetry-space-and-time

Chapter 2

- Milojković, M., MA. (2023, January 30). Nikola Tesla's Strange But Deep Lessons To See Your Life As It Is in 9 Minutes. *Medium.* https://medium.com/fragments-of-history/nikola-teslas-strange-but-deep-lessons-to-see-your-life-as-it-is-in-9-minutes-fb5309d6f44b

- *Nikola Tesla | OCD-UK.* (n.d.). https://www.ocduk.org/ocd/history-of-ocd/nikola-tesla/

Chapter 3

- Lambert, K., Maharishi Mahesh Yogi: The biography of the man who gave transcendental meditation to the world. Doubleday, 1976.
- Farrow, G., & Shearman, C., Transcendental Meditation in America: How a New Age Movement Remade a Small Town in Iowa. University of Iowa Press, 2014.
- Goleman, D., The New York Times Magazine, "Meditation: Shopping for a New Self." November 4, 1979.
- Ospina, MB., Bond K., et al., "Meditation Practices for Health: State of the Research." Evid Rep Technol Assess (Full Rep). 2007 Jun;(155):1-263.
- Chryssides, G., & Wilkins, M., A reader in new religious movements. Continuum International Publishing Group, 2006.
- Obadina, T., "Transcendental Meditation: A Systematic Review of Randomised Controlled Trials." Contemporary Hypnosis, 2019; 36: 235-249.
- Hoge, E. A., Bui, E., Marques, L., Metcalf, C. A., Morris, L. K., Robinaugh, D. J.& Simon, N. M. (2013). Randomized Controlled Trial of Mindfulness Meditation for Generalized Anxiety Disorder: Effects on Anxiety and Stress Reactivity. Journal of Clinical Psychiatry, 74(8), 786-792.
- Tang, Y. Y., Hölzel, B. K., & Posner, M. I. (2015). The neuroscience of mindfulness meditation. Nature Reviews Neuroscience, 16(4), 213-225.

- Jevning, R., Wilson, A. F., & Davidson, J. M. (1978). Adrenocortical activity during meditation. Hormones and Behavior, 10(1), 54-60.

- Boccia, M., Piccardi, L., Guariglia, P., & Giannini, A. M. (2015). Meditation and anxiety: A critical review of the literature. Journal of Cognitive Psychology, 27(3), 257-283.

- Kjaer, T. W., Bertelsen, C., Piccini, P., Brooks, D., Alving, J., & Lou, H. C. (2002). Increased dopamine tone during meditation-induced change of consciousness. Cognitive Brain Research, 13(2), 255-259.

- Brewer, Judson A., et al. "Meditation Experience Is Associated With Differences in Default Mode Network Activity and Connectivity." *Proceedings of the National Academy of Sciences*, vol. 108, no. 50, Nov. 2011, pp. 20254–59. https://doi.org/10.1073/pnas.1112029108.

- Epel, E. S., Puterman, E., Lin, J., Blackburn, E. H., Lum, P. Y., Beckmann, N. D., ... & Mendes, W. B. (2016). Meditation and vacation effects have an impact on disease-associated molecular phenotypes. Translational Psychiatry, 6(8), e880.

- Epel, E., Puterman, E., Lin, J. *et al.* Meditation and vacation effects have an impact on disease-associated molecular phenotypes. *Transl Psychiatry* 6, e880 (2016). https://doi.org/10.1038/tp.2016.164

Chapter 4

- "The Sacred Mushroom and the Cross: A Study of the Nature and Origins of Christianity within the Fertility Cults of the Ancient Near East" by John Marco Allegro. This book explores the theory that early Christianity was influenced by the use of psychedelic mushrooms.

- "The Psychedelic Gospels: The Secret History of Hallucinogens in Christianity" by Jerry B. Brown and Julie M. Brown. This book examines the use of psychedelic substances in the Christian tradition, including the possibility that Jesus and his disciples may have used mushrooms to achieve spiritual insight.
- "The Road to Eleusis: Unveiling the Secret of the Mysteries" by R. Gordon Wasson, Albert Hofmann, and Carl A.P. Ruck. This book explores the use of psychedelic substances in ancient Greek mystery religions, particularly the use of the psychedelic brew known as kykeon in the Eleusinian Mysteries.
- "The Gnostic Bible: Revised and Expanded Edition" edited by Willis Barnstone and Marvin Meyer. This book is a collection of Gnostic texts, including the Gospel of Thomas and the Gospel of Mary, which contain references to mystical experiences and spiritual awakening.
- "How to Change Your Mind: What the New Science of Psychedelics Teaches Us About Consciousness, Dying, Addiction, Depression, and Transcendence" by Michael Pollan. This book explores the current research into the therapeutic potential of psychedelic substances, including psilocybin mushrooms, and their use in spiritual practices.
- Hofmann, A. (1980). The discovery of LSD and subsequent investigations on naturally occurring hallucinogens. Journal of Psychoactive Drugs, 12(1), 7-14.Schultes, R. E., & Hofmann,

A. (1980). Plants of the gods: Origins of hallucinogenic use. McGraw-Hill.Furst, P. T. (1976). Hallucinogens and culture. Chandler & Sharp.

- Stamets, P. (2012). Turkey Tail: The Mushroom of Many Colors. Fungi Magazine, 5(2), 22-25. - This article provides an overview of Turkey Tail mushroom, its historical uses, and its potential in cancer treatment.National Center for Complementary and Integrative Health (NCCIH). (2019). Mushroom Polysaccharides: Cancer Treatment and Beyond. Retrieved from https://www.nccih.nih.gov/health/ mushroom-polysaccharidesLindequist, U., Niedermeyer, T. H., & Jülich, W. D. (2005). The pharmacological potential of mushrooms. Evidence-Based Complementary and Alternative Medicine, 2(3), 285-299.

- Andreae, M. H., Carter, G. M., Shaparin, N., Suslov, K., Ellis, R. J., Ware, M. A., ... & Abrams, D. I. (2015). Inhaled Cannabis for Chronic Neuropathic Pain: A Meta-analysis of Individual Patient Data. The Journal of Pain, 16(12), 1221-1232.Boehnke, K. F., Litinas, E., & Clauw, D. J. (2017). Medical Cannabis Use Is Associated With Decreased Opiate Medication Use in a Retrospective Cross-Sectional Survey of Patients With Chronic Pain. The Journal of Pain, 16(6), 616-624.

- Ayahuasca Churches in America: The Santo Daime and the UDV" - by Alex Gearin (Journal of Contemporary Religion, 2019).

- "Hallucinogens and Religion" - by John A. Rush (Academic Press, 2003)."The Legality of Ayahuasca Religious Use in the United States: An Examination of Gonzales v. O Centro Espirita Beneficente Uniao do Vegetal" - by Rick Strassman (MAPS Bulletin, 2010).

- "Ayahuasca Religions in the United States: Blending Traditional Practice and Modern Sensibility" - by Alex Gearin (Nova Religio: The Journal of Alternative and Emergent Religions, 2019).

- Hallucinogenic Drug Psilocybin Eases Existential Anxiety in People With Life-Threatening Cancer12/02/2016https:// www.hopkinsmedicine.org/news/media/releases/ hallucinogenic_drug_psilocybin_eases_existential_anxiety_ in_people_with_life_threatening_cancer

- "The DMT Nexus" (www.dmt-nexus.me): An online community dedicated to discussing and sharing information about DMT and related substances."The Ethnopharmacologic Search for Psychoactive Drugs" by Dennis J. McKenna, Wade Davis, and Benjamin De Leon-Jones."Phytochemical Guide to Australian Acacias" by William E. Mulder and James A. McDonald.

Chapter 5

- "The Universal One" by Walter Russell - This is the primary work in which Russell presents his cosmological ideas. It outlines his theories on the Universal One, its fundamental principles, and the nature of the universe.

- New International Version (NIV) Bible: https://www. biblegateway.com/versions/New-International-Version-NIV-Bible/

- King James Version (KJV) Bible: https://www.biblegateway.com/versions/King-James-Version-KJV-Bible/
- The New Oxford Annotated Bible with the Apocrypha: New Revised Standard Version (NRSV)

Chapter 6

- The Oxford Handbook of Ancient Egyptian Religion" edited by Donald B. Redford: This comprehensive book covers various aspects of ancient Egyptian religion, including beliefs about the afterlife and reincarnation.
- "The Complete Gods and Goddesses of Ancient Egypt" by Richard H. Wilkinson: While this book primarily focuses on the deities of ancient Egypt, it also provides insights into the religious beliefs and practices of the ancient Egyptians, including their views on the afterlife and reincarnation.
- "The Book of Destinies: Discover the Life You were Born to Live" by Chetan Parkyn and Carola Eastwood - This book introduces the concept of the Human Design system, which includes the idea of soul contracts and their influence on our life's path and purpose.
- "Journey of Souls: Case Studies of Life Between Lives" by Michael Newton - While not focused specifically on soul contracts, this book delves into the concept of life between lives and explores the idea that souls make agreements and plans before incarnating.

Chapter 7

- Book: "Science and the Akashic Field: An Integral Theory of Everything" by Ervin Laszlo

- "The Akashic Experience: Science and the Cosmic Memory Field" edited by Ervin Laszlo and Jude Currivan
- Journal Article: "The Akashic Paradigm: New Science, Human Spirituality, and the Cosmic Memory Field" by Ervin Laszlo
- This article, published in the Journal of Consciousness Exploration & Research, delves into Dr. Laszlo's ideas on the Akashic Paradigm, exploring how the concept of the Akashic Field can bridge science and spirituality.
- Book: "The Self-Actualizing Cosmos: The Akasha Revolution in Science and Human Consciousness" by Ervin Laszlo
- In this book, Dr. Laszlo expands on his theories of the Akashic Field and its transformative potential for human consciousness, drawing on scientific discoveries and spiritual.

Chapter 8

- "The Archetypes and the Collective Unconscious" by Carl Jung: This seminal work by Carl Jung delves into the concept of the collective unconscious. Jung suggests that the collective unconscious is a repository of shared, universal symbols and patterns that are inherited by all individuals. It is a deeper layer of the psyche that connects us to the larger human experience.
- "The Secret of the Golden Flower: A Chinese Book of Life" translated by Richard Wilhelm: This book is a translation of a classic Chinese text that explores the concept of the Alayavijnana, known as the "storehouse consciousness" in Mahayana Buddhism. It discusses the idea of a fundamental consciousness that stores all the impressions and experiences of an individual and influences their thoughts and actions.

- "Synchronicity: An Acausal Connecting Principle" by Carl Jung: In this work, Jung discusses the concept of synchronicity, which refers to meaningful coincidences that occur without any apparent causal connection. He suggests that these synchronistic events are influenced by the collective unconscious and can provide insights into the deeper aspects of reality.

- "The Nature of Consciousness: Essays on the Unity of Mind and Matter" edited by Rupert Spira: This book is a collection of essays by various authors exploring the nature of consciousness from different perspectives, including metaphysics and spirituality. It touches upon the concept of the collective unconscious and its relation to individual consciousness.

- "The Tibetan Book of the Dead" translated by Robert A. F. Thurman: This translation of the Tibetan Buddhist text provides insights into the afterlife and the nature of consciousness. It discusses the Alayavijnana and its role in the process of death and rebirth, emphasizing the interconnectedness of individual consciousness with the larger collective consciousness.

- "The 4-Minute Mile: Historical Perspective" by Andrew M. Lane and Peter R. Terry (Journal of Sport Behavior, 2000): This scholarly article examines the historical context of the 4-minute mile, its psychological implications, and the subsequent breaking of the barrier.

Controversy and Debunking:

- Christopher Chapple 2008 The Hundredth Monkey Revisited
- Brian G Dias, Kerry J Ressler 2013.12.1 Nature Neuroscience 10.1038/nn.3594 https://www.nature.com/articles/nn.3594

- Ravelli AC, van Der Meulen JH, Michels RP, et al. Glucose tolerance in adults after prenatal exposure to famine. Lancet. 1998;351(9097):173-177.
- Roseboom TJ, van der Meulen JH, Osmond C, et al. Coronary heart disease after prenatal exposure to the Dutch famine, 1944-45. Heart. 2000;84(6):595-598.
- Lumey LH, Stein AD, Susser E. Prenatal famine and adult health. Annu Rev Public Health. 2011;32:237-262.

Chapter 10

- American Psychological Association (APA): The APA is a reputable source for information on various psychological concepts, including intuition. They have published articles and papers that discuss the definition, research, and debates surrounding intuition in psychology. Visit the APA website and search for "intuition" to access relevant articles.
- HeartMath Institute Website: The official website of the HeartMath Institute (www.heartmath.org) is likely to have the latest information on their research, publications, and studies related to intuition and heart coherence.
- Scientific Journals: Look for published papers and articles authored by researchers affiliated with the HeartMath Institute in reputable scientific journals. PubMed and Google Scholar are excellent resources to search for academic publications related to intuition and HeartMath research.
- The Human Microbiome Project (HMP): This project, launched by the National Institutes of Health (NIH) in 2008, aimed to characterize the microbial communities found at multiple

human body sites. You can find detailed information about the HMP on the NIH website: https://hmpdacc.org/

- World Health Organization (WHO): The WHO provides information on the impact of the microbiome on human health and disease. Visit their website for health-related insights: https://www.who.int/

Chapter 11

- Tao Te Ching - attributed to Lao Tzu, an ancient Chinese text dating back to the 4th century BCE. It consists of 81 short chapters or verses that contain the teachings and philosophy of Lao Tzu

- "The Taoism Reader" by Thomas Cleary: This book provides an excellent introduction to Taoism, including historical context and transliteration explanations.

- "The Dao of Translation: An East-West Dialogue" by Eva Hung: This book delves into the topic of translation, including the transliteration of Chinese words into English.

- "Taoism" on Wikipedia: https://en.wikipedia.org/wiki/Taoism

- "Wade–Giles" on Wikipedia: https://en.wikipedia.org/wiki/Wade%E2%80%93Giles

- "Pinyin" on Wikipedia: https://en.wikipedia.org/wiki/Pinyin

Made in United States
Troutdale, OR
01/02/2024

16600868R00131